"In most companies employee referrals are the most reliable source for great candidates, but few have really grasped how to run a great employee referral experience. This book provides the much needed blueprint."

Anthony Onesto, SVP People, Suzy

"A practical, informative and engaging guide to one the most important business challenges - finding the right people"

Dr. David Chapman, Deputy Director, UCL School of Management

"Hands-down, the most in-depth publication on referrals which is the secret sauce of the talent underworld. A-Players bring A Players and B-Players bring B- Players to the table. When A-Players are engaged as part of your process, your organization will THRIVE!"

Philip Dana, VP, Talent Acquisition, HR Ops, & Total Rewards, Bridgepoint Education

"There is consensus in the industry that employee referrals is a critical channel for recruiting in-demand talent, but precious little detail on how to effectively go about it, never mind pulling it all in one place. This book solves both of those problems. Must read for any TA pro."

Hung Lee, CEO, Workshape

"A comprehensive overview of arguably the best source of finding new employees."

Todd Raphael, Editor in Chief, ERE Media

"A clear blueprint for any company looking to rapidly scale using one of the most important sources of hire."

Andy McLoughlin OBE, Partner, Uncork Capital

"Actionable, insightful and comprehensive - this is a must-read for teams looking to succeed in their referral programs."

Anj Vera, CEO, TalentView / Author, Rethink Recruitment

"This book can help any organisation - however big or small - master the art of employee referrals"

Taras Polischuk, Managing Partner, HRTechTank

"Finally, an intelligent deep-dive on the one channel that can meaningfully improve the ROI of any company's sourcing efforts"

William Fischer, Previously GM Data Services, DHI Group

"Great book with practical quick tips and ideas that will help recruit employees in the current competitive job market"

Andy Jurczyk, Chief Information Office, Seyfarth Shaw LLP

"Clear, concise and actionable. A must-read guide for anyone looking to quickly improve results from their employee referral program."

Tony Scherba, CEO, Yeti

"Your employees are key to attracting talent in today's competitive recruiting environment. This book will give you the tools and strategies to increase employee engagement and maximize participation in your referral program."

Gokul Rajaram, Caviar Lead, Square

"Talent Knows Talents distills key learnings in employee referral programs, one of the most effective ways for building a successful company and organisational culture, into a practical how to guide."

Thomas Stone, Senior Teaching Fellow, University College London

"This book identifies clear and practical strategies for maximizing how you can leverage employees to attract the best talent to your organization."

David Gildeh, CEO, Outlyer

"If your number one quality source-of-hire is not employee referrals, then you are doing it wrong. This book provides practical insights for any company to enhance its program"

Jer Langhans, Co-founder Paired Sourcing

"A comprehensive and practical guide for any company looking to maximize the ROI of their employee referral program"

Jocelyn Jackson, CFO, Symic Bio

"An invaluable guide for any company looking to develop their employee referral network into a sustainable competitive advantage"

Leon Crutchley, Entrepreneur in Residence, Citi Ventures

"If you are considering implementing or currently operating a recruitment referral program this book tells you everything you need to get the best results"

Shane Gray, EVP Global Business Development, Clinch

"This book is a succint guide of how top performing organizations attract their highest quality talent"

Muz Azar, Founder, SUSO Digital

"Talent Knows Talent is the new go-to resource HR and TA professionals are waiting for. The practical applications are punctuated with the "Did You Know?" and "Quick Wins" suggestions throughout each chapter. Those help make this a fast-hitting guide to how to recognize and take advantage of your employee referrals."

Trish McFarlane, CEO, H3 HR Advisors

"Referrals are one of the most powerful talent sources,yet organizations rarely find ways to improve their programs effectively. Talent Knows Talent provides insights into how to start a journey to take your referrals to the next level."

Gabriele Silva, Senior EMEA Talent Acquisition Manager, VFC

"Employee referrals have always been the backbone of how a successful organization attracts talent. This publication provides a clear guide to help adapt your referral program to the 21st century talent acquisition landscape"

Ronald Cummings-John, Managing Director, Global App Testing

"An Indispensable book for senior executives and founders striving to build a world class talent acquisition function"

Anton Derlyatka, Co-Founder, Sweatcoin and Founding Partner, Talent Equity Ventures

"As more companies take an active approach to their employee referral programs, this book provides a solid framework within which they can quickly and easily make lasting changes"

Dimitar Stanimiroff, CEO, Heresy

"Our best source of candidates is our own employees. Our second-best source of candidates is our employees' connections. This book provides a clear guide on how to optimize your program."

Vicki Foster, Talent Acquisition Manager, Arcadis

"A well-designed employee referral program gives all employees the ability to feel ownership in the hiring process and act as talent scouts to attract the right type of talent. This not only ensures that positions are filled quickly; it also evolves the culture to be one of cooperation, teamwork and empathy."

Caitlin Peake, Director of Talent Acquisition & Employee Experience, RaceTrac Petroleum

TALENT KNOWS TALENT

FIVE EMPLOYEE REFERRAL ELEMENTS
FOR THE MODERN TALENT ACQUISITION PROFESSIONAL

KES THYGESEN
JP BERTRAM
ALESSANDRA WILLIAMS
STEPHEN BROWN

SAN FRANCISCO   LOS ANGELES   PORTLAND
NEW YORK   LONDON

First Edition: October 2018

Content by Kes Thygesen
Design by JP Bertram
Quotes by Alessandra Williams
Proofed by Stephen Brown

ISBN 978-1-7327790-0-6 (paperback)
ISBN 978-1-7327790-1-3 (ebook)

www.RolePoint.com
Printed in PRC

For anyone who's gotten by with a little help from their friends.

CONTENTS

EDUCATION 44

COMMUNICATION 64

TECHNOLOGY 86

CONCLUSION 102

INTRODUCTION

A lot has been written about employee referral programs. Today a search engine query will return more information than any single organization can practically put into practice. It's difficult to know where to start making changes without understanding how a referral program works as a whole. With that in mind, we've condensed our own experience of speaking to more than 2,500 talent practitioners over the past seven years and refined the essence of what makes a great referral program into five actionable elements:

Objectives

Incentives

Education

Communication

Technology

While no single incentive structure or referral policy will fit every organization, the guidelines we've provided for every element will allow you as a talent acquisition professional to evaluate and enhance your program quickly - bringing it in-line with the world's best.

By the end of this book, we hope that you have a high-level understanding of each of the five employee referral program elements and have the tools necessary to put changes into practice. If the phrase 'Talent Knows Talent' resonates and you believe employee referrals to be your strongest source-of-hire, this book will help you master how to consistently generate referral program engagement to attract the highest quality talent.

HOW TO USE THIS BOOK

The focus of this book is practicality. Rather than rehashing countless studies around what makes employee referrals such a great source of hire, we want to give you actionable insights so you can start making positive changes to your referral program today. Don't feel that you need to read the book from start to finish; perhaps there's an element of your program you think needs work and that's where you have the buy-in to begin making changes.

There's a checklist at the end of every section to allow you to grade your program on the most universally important criteria (these are also summarized on page 118). We've structured the text to contain a variety of call-out boxes to make the information easily accessible:

 Top 5 Questions. We surveyed talent acquisition practitioners to find out which questions were most important for them to answer for each of the five elements. Every chapter starts by outlining these questions.

 **Graph.** As part of the primary research for this book, we surveyed 1,000 people working in talent acquisition on their referral program. These results help you baseline against other organizations' programs.

Quote. We conducted long-form interviews with over 30 talent acquisition leaders to share first-hand ideas on what's currently working effectively at their organization.

 Quick Wins. Low cost, fast changes you can implement at your organization today to start generating results.

 **Explore Further.** For every element, there are links to online content. Frequently these are templated referral program assets that can quickly be adapted for use at your organization.

 Did You Know? Interesting facts around referral programs to support internal discussions.

Checklist. Five checklist items are provided for every element to help you evaluate your current referral program. On page 114, you can grade your program out of a maximum score of twenty-five.

OBJECTIVES

"OUR GOALS CAN ONLY BE REACHED THROUGH A VEHICLE OF A PLAN, IN WHICH WE MUST FERVENTLY BELIEVE, AND UPON WHICH WE MUST VIGOROUSLY ACT. THERE IS NO OTHER ROUTE TO SUCCESS."

PABLO PICASSO

When implementing your employee referral program (ERP), it's essential you set goals to determine what success looks like for your company. Talent acquisition thrives when you measure your practices, track your progress, and make adjustments to continually improve your strategy.

The first step is setting objectives.

A set-it-and-forget-it approach falls flat. It's important to focus on efficiency and to optimize your efforts -- otherwise, your ERP becomes stagnant.

In this chapter, we will cover the most commonly asked questions related to the first element of successful ERPs -- objectives. Employers looking to optimize their ERP want to know:

What percentage of hires come from employee referrals?

Referrals are the reigning champions for quality of hire. We will explore their prevalence and what portion of hires they typically comprise.

What is the average cost-per-hire of employee referrals versus other sources?

From job board postings to social recruiting, every source of hire carries a cost. We will examine the costs of some of the most common sources of hire and how employee referrals compare.

> The oldest employee referral program dates back to Roman times. A decree signed by Julius Caesar in 55 B.C. promised a reward of 300 sestertii to any soldier who brought another to join the Roman army. The amount represented a third of a soldier's annual pay. They had the first known recruiters and faced many of the same talent acquisition challenges we have today.
>
> **DID YOU KNOW?**

What stats should I track as part of a successful referral program?

Data is essential in determining the success of your ERP. We will uncover the most important metrics you should be measuring and why they matter.

How can I support diversity and veteran hiring using the referral program?

A common goal for many companies is generating diversity through their ERP. We will show how referral programs support your diversity hiring agenda.

How can I leverage our employee base to build our employer brand?

The employer brand is the foundation of a successful referral program. We will identify practical strategies you can use to get your passionate workforce involved in building an attractive employer brand.

I. WHAT PERCENTAGE OF HIRES COME FROM EMPLOYEE REFERRALS?

STUDY: What percentage of your new hires comes from employee referrals?

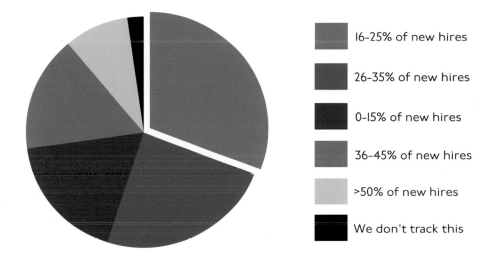

- 16-25% of new hires
- 26-35% of new hires
- 0-15% of new hires
- 36-45% of new hires
- >50% of new hires
- We don't track this

Referrals continue as the top source of hire, bringing in 30 percent of all hires in 2016.[1]

The employee referral continues to thrive as the leading source of hire for many organizations for one reason -- it is the top channel for best quality of hire.[2]

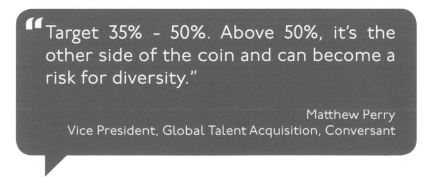

❝Target 35% - 50%. Above 50%, it's the other side of the coin and can become a risk for diversity."

Matthew Perry
Vice President, Global Talent Acquisition, Conversant

Research found that referrals stand out from other candidates in three areas:

> **Time to start:** candidates hired from referrals start an average of 10 days sooner than other sources of hire.

> **Loyalty:** 47 percent of referral hires stayed at the company for three years or more, compared to just 14 percent of job board hires.

> **Cultural fit:** 70 percent of employers say referred hires fit the company culture and values better than those from other sources of hire.[3]

Another significant advantage to referrals - the conversion rate is high. 40 percent of all candidates who come through referrals are hired, but only 7 percent of applications come from referrals. To put that into perspective: almost half of an organization's hires are made from just 7 percent of the applications they receive.[4]

> **"**This depends on the maturity of the company. For early stage companies having over 50% is not necessarily a bad thing. For companies that are past their growth stage and reaching maturity 20%-30% is the right level to ensure diversity."
>
> Grant Weinberg
> Global Talent Acquisition Leader, Gilead Sciences

This isn't surprising when you step into the shoes of a job seeker. The primary way people find jobs is also through referrals. A simple share leads to big talent wins. This even applies to passive job seekers. In fact, a whopping 87 percent of passive and active candidates are open to new job opportunities.[5]

Internal hiring also benefits from referrals -- 45 percent of internal hires come from referrals, making it the top source of internal hires.[6]

Of course, another major benefit of employee referrals is cost-effectiveness.

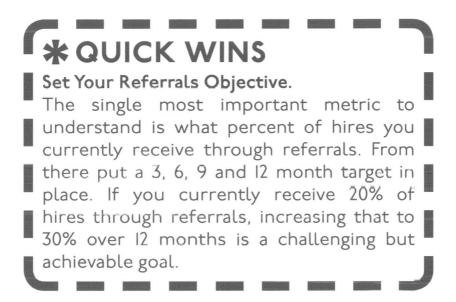

✳ QUICK WINS

Set Your Referrals Objective.
The single most important metric to understand is what percent of hires you currently receive through referrals. From there put a 3, 6, 9 and 12 month target in place. If you currently receive 20% of hires through referrals, increasing that to 30% over 12 months is a challenging but achievable goal.

2. WHAT IS THE AVERAGE COST-PER-HIRE OF EMPLOYEE REFERRALS VERSUS OTHER SOURCES?

Cost to hire is crucial to your recruiting budget. After adding your external and internal costs, divide the sum by the total number of hires during that time period and you have your magic number.

In 2016, the average cost-per-hire was $4,129. As you can imagine, this changes over time and will vary depending on each source of hire.

Recruiters. This is one of the most expensive sources. External recruiters often charge a fee of between 15-25 percent of the candidate's first-year annual earnings. These fees can add up, in some cases averaging over $18,000.[7]

Also, because they're not technically a part of your organization, you risk quality of hire.

STUDY: What are your three sources with the lowest cost-per-hire?

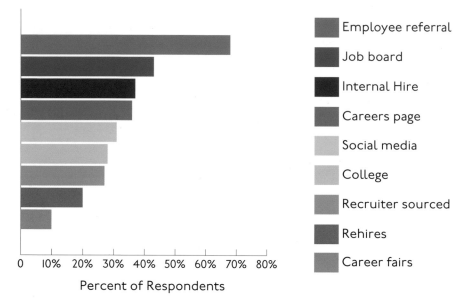

Percent of Respondents

Job Board. Job boards like Indeed lead in pulling in the most interviews.[8] Prices vary between services, but they climb high for premium job boards.

Between advertising and job boards, many companies spend 30 percent of their entire budget.[9]

Internal Hire. Hiring from within saves costs because you already know the cultural fit of current employees, making it easier to screen these candidates.

Referrals. The cost of an employee referral program seems high up-front, but when you consider the advantages you get from referred candidates, the cost-per-hire is significantly lower. In fact, 51 percent of employers said it was less expensive to recruit via referrals.[10]

> " We look at the savings we get from a referral versus hiring someone from an agency. If we hired someone and the agency cost was twenty-four thousand but we just paid two thousand dollars for that referral, then we just saved twenty-two thousand dollars. This highlights the value that is generated not just from referrals but also having an in-house specialist group of talent acquisition versus being dependent on agencies."
>
> George Smallwood
> Director, Talent Acquisition, Ingram Content Group

3. WHAT STATS SHOULD I TRACK AS PART OF A SUCCESSFUL REFERRAL PROGRAM?

A successful ERP helps you hire better people in a faster, more cost-effective way. To ensure the success of your program, measure the following metrics:

Number of referrals from each employee. The number of referred candidates you receive from each individual.

In other words, you're looking at how engaging your ERP is. If each employee is participating and referring a number of talented candidates, this shows you're promoting your program effectively. However, if these numbers are low, it's time to change your communications strategy.

»EXPLORE FURTHER

The Implications of Big Data on Employee Referrals and Recruiting whitepaper at https://rlpt.co/BigDataWhitepaper.

Application completion rate. The number of referred candidates who are actually submitting applications.

If you're noticing a low percentage of referrals completing an application, take a hard look at your application process. Remember, at this stage, the candidate is already aware of an opportunity. Why aren't they applying? It might be a poor candidate experience or a lackluster employer brand.

Employee-referred conversion. The number of employee-referred applicants who get hired.

This indicates how well referred candidates interview and fit into the culture and the role. If you're hiring a large percentage of referred candidates, your employees who are making the referrals have a keen understanding of what the company needs in talent.

Quality of hire. An overall assessment of the new hire viewed through performance reviews, productivity measures, retention, and satisfaction from management.

This is usually the shining star for referred candidates. If your ERP yields low-quality hires, identify where the issue lies. It could be caused by your employees not understanding the company's needs or a flawed hiring process.

Retention rates. The number of employees who stay onboard in a given period of time.

Referrals typically show more loyalty than other hires. If they're jumping ship quickly, your program might not be educating your employees on the importance of cultural fit. Also, you'll need to evaluate how you present job descriptions and management's ability to empower their staff.

STUDY: What are the three most important metrics you track for your ERP?

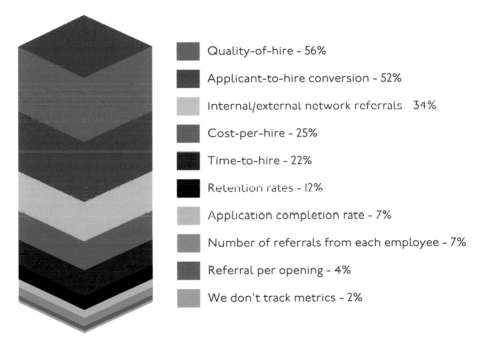

Quality-of-hire - 56%

Applicant-to-hire conversion - 52%

Internal/external network referrals 34%

Cost-per-hire - 25%

Time-to-hire - 22%

Retention rates - 12%

Application completion rate - 7%

Number of referrals from each employee - 7%

Referral per opening - 4%

We don't track metrics - 2%

4. HOW CAN I SUPPORT DIVERSITY AND VETERAN HIRING USING THE REFERRAL PROGRAM

Diversity hiring continues to be a top priority - 51 percent of companies are focusing on diversity for a variety of reasons, including:

- To improve their culture
- To improve their company performance
- To better represent their customers

Their biggest barrier -- finding diverse candidates to interview.[11]

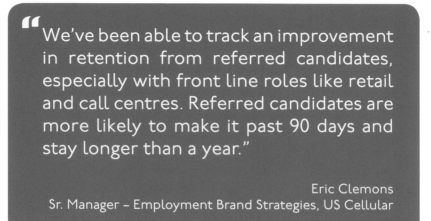

> We've been able to track an improvement in retention from referred candidates, especially with front line roles like retail and call centres. Referred candidates are more likely to make it past 90 days and stay longer than a year."
>
> Eric Clemons
> Sr. Manager – Employment Brand Strategies, US Cellular

Referrals set you apart and contribute to your diversity hiring goals. Follow these strategies:

Added bonuses. Put your money where your mouth is. Instead of talking about the value of diverse talent, show it by offering a bigger financial incentive for quality diversity referrals. This diverse referral bonus sends a clear message -- you're serious about building a more inclusive team.

Management training. Use diversity scorecards to rank managers on how well they recruit and retain diverse talent. This encourages them to be more supportive and proactive in encouraging more diverse referrals. Train them on how to help their employees find and attract diverse talent.

Toolkit. Educate your staff on how to refer diverse candidates successfully. Create a toolkit to teach employees how to:

- Promote features of your company that are attractive to diverse candidates
- Share real testimonials and stories targeted at different diverse groups
- Connect and engage with diverse networks online and in-person

✳ QUICK WINS

Run A Veteran Hiring Campaign.
Run a raffle for every referral submitted that is veteran qualified. See a template campaign here: https://rlpt.co/EmployeeReferralTemplateCampaign

Targeted campaigns. Speak directly to the diverse groups you want to recruit. These groups can center on gender, race, age, educational level, and more. Look for ways to get your employees involved in branding for diversity referral campaigns. For example, share employee testimonial videos highlighting your inclusive culture.

✳ QUICK WINS

Run A Diversity Hiring Campaign.
Double your cash bonus for diversity qualified hires. See a template campaign here: https://rlpt.co/EmployeeReferralTemplateCampaign

Also, create an employee resource group (ERG) for specific populations, like veterans. An ERG for veterans gives your current veteran employees a network within your culture. They can work together to set veteran hiring goals with HR and create an effective veteran referral campaign.

5. HOW CAN I LEVERAGE OUR EMPLOYEE BASE TO BUILD OUR EMPLOYER BRAND?

Companies with successful referral programs have excellent employer branding, thanks in large part to their awesome culture. Simply put, if your staff doesn't love working for you, they won't want to refer others.

Employer branding comes as an afterthought to many employers. Therefore, it's often overlooked in budgeting.

While nearly 70 percent of recruiting budgets go to job boards, recruiting tools, and staffing agencies, talent leaders identify employer branding as the No. 1 area where they wish they could invest more.[12]

The good news is, you don't have to invest big to build a strong employer brand. Your employees are your best resource for branding.

Share the love. Encourage your staff to leave reviews on resources like Glassdoor. They do it anonymously, so they don't have to worry about any backlash from leadership.

Set clear goals for reaching a specific number of Glassdoor reviews, then host a special event to thank your staff for their honest feedback. Show referred candidates you care by publicly responding to reviews, thanking employees who leave positive or constructive reviews, and offering solutions or resolutions when you come across negative feedback.

Get social. When you create employer branding content, like a video explaining your company mission and values, reward employees who share it on their social media. This helps expand your reach.

Also, make it fun by hosting silly group photo contests. Reward the groups who create and share the best photos or gifs they take in the workplace.

Coach and train. Host personal branding sessions for employees to fully develop their online presence on sites like Linkedin. Teach them how to share their expertise. When referrals see your employees showcase their skills and knowledge, they will associate your company with creating strong employees.

» EXPLORE FURTHER

The Social Referral whitepaper at
https://rlpt.co/TheSocialReferral.

Target groups. Encourage employees to target specific social media groups that focus on a profession or your industry. They can connect with groups through several platforms. For example, your software engineers can connect with their colleagues on engineer-specific groups through Linkedin. They can also answer questions on popular platforms like Quora and Reddit.

> "Based on more than a decade of research I can confidently say that a prospect interested in applying for a job in the US should NEVER do so without first obtaining a referral from an employee inside that same company."
>
> Gerry Crispin, Principal & Co-Founder, CareerXroads

✓ CHECKLIST: OBJECTIVES

- [ ] We know what percentage of hires we currently receive through referrals as a source

- [ ] We have a defined target percentage of hires we want through referrals over the next 12 months

- [ ] We have a defined budget of how much we want to spend on the referral program in the next 12 months

- [ ] We have an understanding of which departments/locations we need to generate more referrals in

- [ ] We have strategic recruiting goals (diversity/veteran/campus/employer branding) and can tie this to the referral program

INCENTIVES

"PEOPLE WORK FOR MONEY BUT GO THE EXTRA MILE FOR RECOGNITION, PRAISE, AND REWARDS."

DALE CARNEGIE

Hit your ERP objectives by creating a varied, robust incentives strategy. While bonuses and prizes shouldn't be the primary motivating factor for employees, they still play a big part in boosting engagement.

In this chapter, we will explore the most commonly asked questions about incentives:

How much cash should I pay out for successful referrals?

Financial incentives do work to a degree, but there is no 'right' answer. We will determine the role cash plays in your program and debunk the myth that more money yields more referrals.

What policy on probation periods should be associated with incentives?

Patience is a virtue, but you can't expect employees to wait forever for their incentives. We will look at how to create a policy that's right for you and uncover how to keep employees engaged and motivated.

Should I reward for participation in the program along with successful hires?

The easy answer is yes. We will uncover the two biggest frustrations your employees face and how to create participation-based incentives.

What non-cash rewards work well?

Cash is just one component of your referral program incentives. We will offer ideas for various kinds of non-cash rewards. This ensures all employees, including those who aren't primarily motivated by cash, are engaged.

How can social recognition and gamification be used?

These are some of the most powerful motivating factors. We will determine how to gamify your program and also use social recognition to get your staff excited to participate.

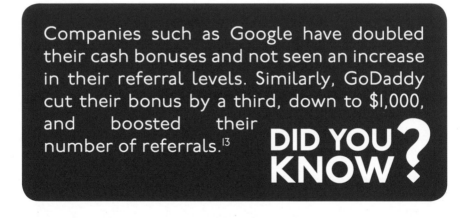

Companies such as Google have doubled their cash bonuses and not seen an increase in their referral levels. Similarly, GoDaddy cut their bonus by a third, down to $1,000, and boosted their number of referrals.[13] **DID YOU KNOW?**

I. HOW MUCH CASH SHOULD I PAY OUT FOR SUCCESSFUL REFERRALS?

The short answer is: it depends.

There are several variables to consider when you're structuring your cash incentives, including country, industry, and seniority of the position.

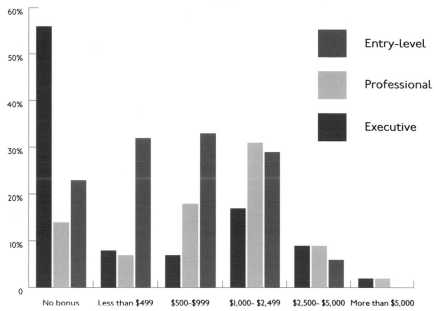

STUDY: How much do you pay out for referral bonuses upon a successful hire?

Entry-level
Professional
Executive

No bonus   Less than $499 $500-$999 $1,000- $2,499 $2,500- $5,000   More than $5,000

Here's a quick look at average referral bonuses:

Incentives vary widely, ranging from $50 to more than $20,000. The most common range is between $1,000 and $2,500. However, some companies offer much more.

Inbound marketing and sales platform, Hubspot, for example, offers a $10,000 referral bonus for adding full-time developers and designers to their team.[14]

Your cash incentive strategy should clearly state how much employees can expect, as well as identify who is eligible. Certain employees, like hiring managers, recruiters, and senior leadership, should not be eligible.

On the other hand, consider engaging vendors, contractors, consultants, and former employees in your program.

> **"**The reward balance is really important. We started with a very standardized reward methodology that was consistent across the globe. There are certain regions in the world where a large dollar amount referral bonus is incredibly attractive versus reasonably attractive. On paper that seems like a really positive thing, right? We are going to be paying a large amount for a referral in India or Latin America, two low-cost regions, the downside is that is distorts the true value of a referral. We have people in Latin America that were potentially earning as much through the referral bonuses as their annual salary, that was making them do some strange things like going out almost on street corners finding people. Getting the balance right for rewards, particularly internationally, is crucial."
>
> Shane Hicks, VP Global Talent, Epicor

Employers are expanding their referral programs to allow non-employees to submit referrals. HR thought leader Dr. John Sullivan calls this "friends of the firm" referrals (FOF). This gives you more talent scouts on the ground and can lead to high-quality candidates who are outside of your typical set of prospects.

Some critics insist that cash incentives don't drive more referrals or bring in higher quality candidates. There are examples of high profile companies both increasing and decreasing their referral bonuses without the expected impact on referral rates.

> **"**Most of the time people aren't referring for the money, they're referring because they want to help the company or they want to help that person and they feel like they're genuinely a good fit. We wouldn't recommend a bonus over $2,500. There's a certain point where the cash amount is enough inspiration to refer people and the motivation gains beyond that are minimal."
>
> Neil Costa, Founder & CEO, HireClix

There are various reasons why using only cash bonuses is not effective:

Lack of ongoing engagement. Lump sum bonuses don't create much motivation. Once a referrer is paid, they're unlikely to continue to submit referrals.

A disappearing prize. Many employees who receive cash are likely to just add it to their bank account, where it is used for everyday living expenses.

Different personalities. Not every employee is motivated by cash. Motivation depends on each person's unique personality.

Combine drivers, like altruistic incentives, intrinsic motivators, and various financial rewards. This way, employees with different personality types will want to participate.

✳ QUICK WINS

Double your referral bonus for 30 days for 5 hard-to-fill roles. A temporary increase in referral bonus is a great way to get your employees' attention and incentivize them to start submitting candidates today. Doing this only for hard-to-fill roles helps focus their efforts on high value areas of their network.

See a template campaign here: https://rlpt. co/EmployeeReferralTemplateCampaign

2. WHAT PROBATION PERIODS AND POLICY SHOULD BE ASSOCIATED WITH INCENTIVES?

"We reduced our probation period from 90 to 30 days to help reinforce the trust in the referral program - for the most part whether the candidate stays or not after hire is out of the employees' hands."

Justin Copp
Senior Manager, Global Talent Acquisition, PayPal

Failing to provide employees with feedback on submitted referrals creates a black hole. Don't leave your employees in the dark. If your probation periods are lengthy and you're not continually engaging referrers, you're going to see a drop in participation.

Withholding incentives during the probationary period is problematic. While you want to ensure referred candidates stay onboard and dissuade employees from exploiting the referral program, withholding incentives creates several issues.

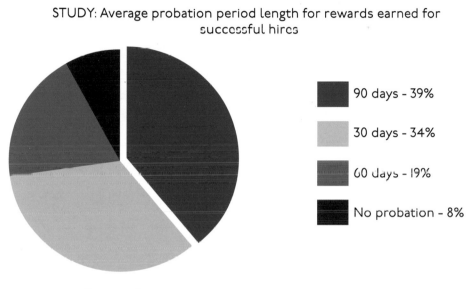

STUDY: Average probation period length for rewards earned for successful hires

- 90 days - 39%
- 30 days - 34%
- 60 days - 19%
- No probation - 8%

Respondents

This approach implies:

- You don't trust employees to screen and submit quality referrals.
- You think employees don't realize that a bad referral reflects poorly on them.
- You don't trust hiring managers to onboard candidates who will positively impact your business results.

Additionally, withholding incentives will make the reward less impactful. If your main concern is employees taking advantage by focusing on quantity over quality, it's best to approach that situation or employee on an individual basis.

STUDY: Who is not eligible for referral program bonuses?

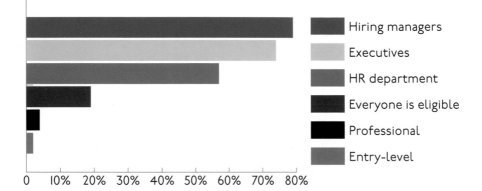

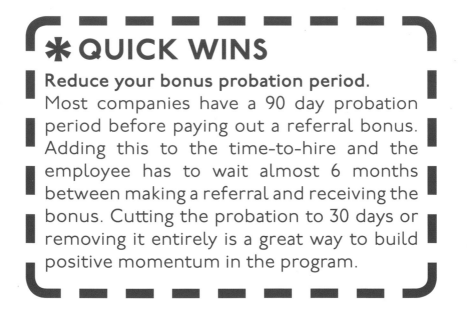

✳ QUICK WINS

Reduce your bonus probation period.
Most companies have a 90 day probation period before paying out a referral bonus. Adding this to the time-to-hire and the employee has to wait almost 6 months between making a referral and receiving the bonus. Cutting the probation to 30 days or removing it entirely is a great way to build positive momentum in the program.

It's also unfair to suggest that employees need to guarantee long-term tenure for referrals. They're not recruiters. Their role in the referral program is to submit high-quality candidates they think will thrive in the culture and the prospective role.

Employees don't have control over whether their contacts stay or not, so consider removing probation periods for referrals. They should be praised for their efforts, regardless of the success of the candidate.

If you insist on enforcing a probation period, keep it shorter than 90 days. Also, consider offering smaller rewards from time-to-hire to the end of the probation period.

Another aspect of your incentive policy you need to address is managing duplicate referrals. What happens if several employees submit the same candidate for a job?

» EXPLORE FURTHER
You can view a template 'Employee Referral Program Policy' on page 116 (https://rlpt.co/SampleEmployeeReferralPolicy).

Your employees might know and refer the same candidates if they share the same talent networks. While unexpected, this is a possible scenario so make sure you have a policy in place to head off any major disputes.

This is why a good referral tracking program is essential. When an employee submits an email address for the duplicate referral, the software will alert the referrer that the email already exists in the system.

One of the best ways to address duplicate referrals that make it through the initial screening is establishing a first come, first serve rule. Consider a policy that works for your budget and your culture.

Once you establish rules and policies for your incentives, host a 'get to know your incentives' meeting to share them with your staff. Then, demonstrate how employees can access the policies through an online portal. This way, it's clear what they can expect to see with the referral program experience.

3. SHOULD I REWARD FOR PARTICIPATION IN THE PROGRAM ALONG WITH SUCCESSFUL HIRES?

Giving bonuses for 'qualified referrals' is very effective. A qualified referral is someone who makes it to the first interview. At this

> "I have never really seen a different output based on increased cash bonuses. What I find is more effective is the participation based reward - an immediate reward for effort. As an employee I can only impact who I refer, after that it's out of my control. It's a recruiter or the hiring manager or timing, they'll then decide the fate of that referral. If I know I'll get a $10 Starbucks gift card or a movie pass or a dinner coupon for submitting a referral, it's different - it's immediate. If I don't end up with the cash, I don't mind - I've helped my friend out and done something good for the company."
>
> Kevin Benton, Head of Americas
> Talent Acquisition & Global Executive Search, McAfee

> **"**We run monthly email campaigns and have quarterly leaderboards tracked by a point system based on referral actions. We also reward participation where we choose 2 people who have made at least a single referral. We reward them with raffle prizes like Apple Airpods or Amazon Echos."
>
> Melissa Ngo-Harris, Recruiting Manager, Aptos Retail

STUDY: When do you reward employees who submit referrals?

After the referral completes the probation period - 78%

After the referral is submitted for consideration - 23%

Once the referral makes it to the first interview - 18%

When the referral is hired - 15%

stage, the referrer deserves an incentive for submitting a strong candidate.

✳ QUICK WINS

Run a referral raffle to reward participation. For every referral that is submitted that makes it to a first round interview, give the employee a raffle ticket. Send out updates once a week for four weeks and then have a drawing for a winner. Experiences or luxury gift prizes work really well, consider local sports tickets, high-end tech gadgets or unique trips such as helicopter rides.

See example raffle campaigns here: https://rlpt.co/EmployeeReferralsPlaybook

These participation-based bonuses fuel engagement and boost referrals-per-employee. This helps build a culture of referrals. By adding recognition to the referral process, you're delivering a powerful message to employees - they have a hand in creating a positive community in the company.

Social recognition is a valuable, inexpensive method for boosting engagement and participation. For example, a hiring manager delivers a personal thank-you note or the referrer is named in the company newsletter. Showing appreciation for their efforts communicates how much your company values quality referrals.

Other simple ways to boost participation include:

- Promoting big-picture ideas from your company to increase pride and excitement
- Establishing a referral meeting schedule with top performers
- Teaching new hires the importance of the referral program during the orientation process
- Updating your referral program theme and branding regularly to keep it exciting
- Adopting a 'recruiting culture' mentality and earn buy-in from all levels of management

Participation-based rewards deliver positive feedback quickly, which encourages even more referrals.

4. WHAT NON-CASH REWARDS WORK WELL?

> "Trips, raffles for popular technology products, charity donations. There aren't necessarily incentives for executives, but there have been charity donations done on their behalf to the charity of their choice."
>
> Jennifer Picard, Partner, KMA Talent Solutions

Building an incentive strategy should include rewards that are relevant to all kinds of personalities. Some employees want more than cash. They are motivated by contributing to charities, pursuing unique experiences, and other tangible rewards.

Here are a few different kinds of non-cash incentives:

Participation-based rewards or micro-rewards. Use these for when employees submit referrals and for successful hires. Examples include:

- Gym memberships
- Subscription services (Spotify, Amazon Prime, Apple Music, etc.)
- Tickets (sporting events, live theatre, cinema, etc.)
- Gift cards for necessities (gas, groceries, etc.)
- Gift cards for fun (spa, coffee shops, restaurants, travel, iTunes, etc.)

> "We've used gift-cards, prizes like gym memberships and partnered with companies like Southwest to give points away. For successful hires, employees can take a cash bonus or we'll double the amount to donate to a charity they're passionate about."
>
> Bethany Parthun
> Corporate HR Manager, Talent, Evolution Hospitality

Raffle campaigns. Seasonal giveaways should include raffle tickets for every qualified referral (e.g. a referral that makes it to a first-round interview). Consider the time of the year when selecting seasonal campaigns for raffles. Examples include:

- Dinner cruise
- Hot air balloon rides
- Sporting event tickets
- Music festival tickets
- Golf at an exclusive course

Draw winners at a company-wide meeting, then use the employee's trip experience as content to promote your next campaign.

Charity rewards. These altruistic rewards motivate those who are driven by helping others. Examples include:

- Plant a tree with Plant a Billion
- Feed the Children -- feed a child for a year
- Rainforest Alliance -- adopt a rainforest
- Donations for various causes

STUDY: Non-cash rewards you offer for referrals

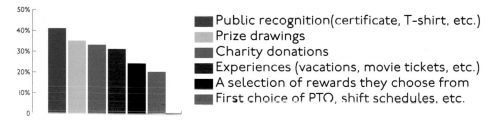

Public recognition(certificate, T-shirt, etc.)
Prize drawings
Charity donations
Experiences (vacations, movie tickets, etc.)
A selection of rewards they choose from
First choice of PTO, shift schedules, etc.

STUDY: Our employees are motivated by our referral program incentives

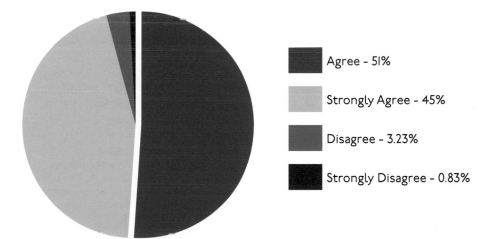

Agree - 51%

Strongly Agree - 45%

Disagree - 3.23%

Strongly Disagree - 0.83%

International rewards. Global companies should consider what resonates with employees who live in different areas of the world. Examples include:

- Helicopter ride over New York
- Charter boats in Hong Kong
- Cruise in Venice, Italy
- Breakfast at Taj Mahal

✳ QUICK WINS

Run a charity donation based referral campaign. For every referral that is submitted, make a small donation in that employee's name to a charity the organization supports. Often high-profile newsworthy topics such as a disaster relief effort are a timely cause that it's easy to get employees to take action for. Send out updates once a week for four weeks, highlighting the employees who have made the most referrals. Potentially introduce an added reward for the employee that has made the most referrals and celebrate how much you have raised at the end.

View a template charity campaign here:
https://rlpt.co/
EmployeeReferralTemplateCampaign

> **"** Instead of rewarding participation with incentives like gift-cards, we give out points that employees can redeem for cash prizes, gifts, travel incentives and lots of other rewards. There's something that appeals to everybody and they can easily keep earning points over time participating in the referral program and other company wide initiatives."
>
> Brooke Glennon, Associate Director, Recruitment
> Marketing & Operations, Encompass Health

Social rewards. Publicly praising employees is sufficient for those who are driven by social motivation. Examples include:

- Top referrer swag (mug, shirt, trophy, etc.)
- Recognition postcards
- Day out of the office
- Thank you gift at desk
- Top referrers leaderboard

» EXPLORE FURTHER

See a broad range of non-cash referral program reward options including charity, micro-rewards and experiences in this *'101 Ideas for Employee Referrals Rewards'* presentation: https://rlpt.co/101RewardIdeas

> "Once a quarter we have 'Conversant Wins' to celebrate successes. This is a company wide global discussion where we highlight who's been the top referrers and which department generated the most referrals to introduce some friendly competition."
>
> Matthew Perry
> Vice President of Global Talent Acquisition, Conversant

Social recognition fuels a recruiting-focused culture, which is a big advantage. You want to get employees excited about thinking like talent scouts.

> "Some employees thrive off the camaraderie of competitiveness and trying to be at the top of the leaderboard or the star for most referrals that quarter. That creates strong engagement and buzz without even having a monetary value."
>
> Michelle Sargent
> Head of Strategic Partnerships, KRT Marketing

There are several ways to drive social recognition. For example, distribute company swag (t-shirts, coffee mugs, etc.) with fun phrases, like 'Referral Master.' Hand out Olympic-style medals once every quarter and host a public event to praise the top three best referrers.

Other fun ways to drive social recognition include appointing referral program ambassadors. Encourage them to develop and lead fun, culture-specific ceremonies to praise successful referrers. Be sure to make it unique to your culture so it resonates with employees.

✳ QUICK WINS

Publish a referral leaderboard.
Employees love to be recognized. Publish a monthly leaderboard of the top 10 employees who've made the most referrals. If you're a large organization, do this for every department. At the end of every quarter, have the senior management team recognize the person who's made the most referred hires.

View this referral campaign hub to learn more about referral leaderboards: https://learn.rolepoint.com/campaigns

Another great approach is to implement gamification into your program. To gamify your referral process, focus on making the employee experience simple, straightforward, and fun. You should use real-time recognition with this strategy as well.

Creating a points-based system is the best way to drive partici-pation through gamification. Employees complete specific referral tasks to earn points and add to their total. For example, if they share a job posting on their social media account, they receive 20 points. For every view their referral-link gains, they can earn an additional point.

Also, create and post live leaderboards for everyone to track. This drives friendly competition that is both fun and engaging.

≫EXPLORE FURTHER

To learn more about how leading companies have used rewards and recognition to drive engagement in their employee referral programs check out this *'Gamification in Referrals and Recruitment Whitepaper'*: https://rlpt.co/GamificationWhitepaper

✔CHECKLIST: INCENTIVES

☐ We offer cash rewards for successful rewards (success based bonuses)

☐ Our probation period for referred hires is no more than 90 days

☐ We offer non-cash rewards for employees submitting qualified referrals (participation based bonuses)

☐ We have the flexibility to run campaigns with temporary bonuses (gift-cards/raffle prizes/charity donations)

☐ We use social recognition to highlight top performing referrers

EDUCATION

"GOOD TEACHING IS MORE A GIVING OF RIGHT QUESTIONS THAN A GIVING OF RIGHT ANSWERS."

JOSEF ALBERS

An educated workforce is your best tool for your ERP. If your team is not informed about your employee referral objectives or aware of the incentives they can earn, your program will be stagnant.

In this chapter, we cover the most commonly asked questions about education:

How do I get employees to care about employee referrals?

The perfect process for your ERP doesn't guarantee participation. We will look at the value of simplicity and show how to make referrals a priority for your entire staff.

How do I educate employees on where to submit referrals?

Employees can't help you hit your referral objectives if they don't know how to participate. We will explore why teaching employees early is important and how to engage them in education continually.

How can line-managers help drive employee participation?

Management has a direct influence on their team. We will determine the best practices for managers to engage their employees on an ongoing basis.

How do I brand my employee referral program?

Brands create engagement. We will identify branding strategies that you can market to your employees to get them excited about contributing to your program.

How do I get employees to focus on quality referrals?

Quality always beats quantity. Don't settle for subpar referred candidates. We will reveal the best ways to communicate your candidate preferences to employees.

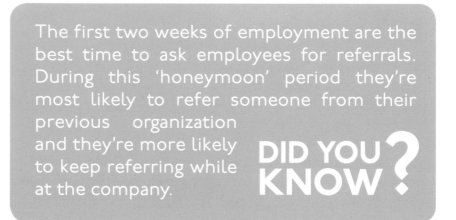

The first two weeks of employment are the best time to ask employees for referrals. During this 'honeymoon' period they're most likely to refer someone from their previous organization and they're more likely to keep referring while at the company.

DID YOU KNOW?

I. HOW DO I GET EMPLOYEES TO CARE ABOUT EMPLOYEE REFERRALS?

Motivation is tricky, especially when you're asking your employees to act as talent scouts on top of their daily responsibilities. While incentives play a big part, the most effective way to get employees to care about submitting referrals is to show them the benefits of referrals.

> "One of the biggest barriers to referrals is employees getting nervous that they're attached to candidates who may not always be a good hire. The employee education process is really important to remove this psychological barrier - to make employees comfortable with referring and getting across the message that they won't be held accountable for the contacts they are introducing."
>
> Grant Weinberg
> Global Talent Acquisition Leader, Gilead Sciences

You know the many benefits of hiring referred candidates -- less time to hire, more likely to stay longer, higher quality of hire, and much more. Now share the benefits your employees reap when they refer the best of the best.

> "It's very important to have someone dedicated to the referral program when an organization gets to a certain size. There is usually a need for single point of contact to partner internally with the comms team, marketing and talent acquisition to continue driving employee engagement."
>
> Justin Copp
> Senior Manager, Global Talent Acquisition, PayPal

> **"**Sometimes associates are hesitant to refer because they feel that if their contact isn't a perfect fit, it may look bad on them. Getting the message across that their candidate introductions alone are really valuable can help alleviate these concerns and make employees more comfortable with referring."
>
> Fatima Qizilbas
> Manager, Talent Marketing, LoyaltyOne

The most obvious benefit is that they have the chance to select who they work alongside. By referring people they know possess a strong work ethic and who fit the culture, they can see the short and long-term advantages: a more productive workforce, potential for higher bonuses, a boost in job security, and continued company growth.

STUDY: Which strategic initiatives have you supported through your ERP?

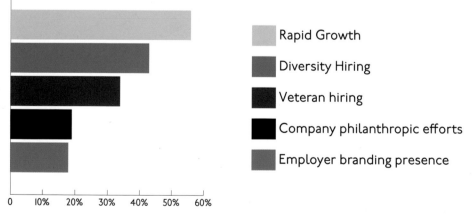

Rapid Growth

Diversity Hiring

Veteran hiring

Company philanthropic efforts

Employer branding presence

0   10%   20%   30%   40%   50%   60%

Percent of Respondents

After showing them why they should care about helping build your team, make it easy for them to participate. Do not make the policy overly complicated. Keep the rules and the process simple.

> **"**At the end of the first year of running the program we reached out to people who had submitted a referral to ask their advice on what prizes they liked, what they didn't like and what they would like to see more of. We received a lot of feedback that it should be smaller rewards for activity and not necessarily for people to get hired. Involving the employees in this process was a great way to get them more bought into the program."
>
> Nadine Lou
> Talent Acquisition Specialist, MarketSource

They will care more about submitting candidates if you guide them. Instruct them on how to build their referral network online, through social media, and through in-person networking opportunities. Consider paying for their memberships to various professional organizations where they can meet colleagues in your industry.

Also, make referrals a part of the entire performance management process. This way, when leadership conducts performance reviews throughout the year, employees assess their referral goals and keep the conversation going on how to achieve those goals.

If you notice a lack of engagement, employees probably will not feel comfortable referring candidates. Some employees assume if their referral doesn't get the job or becomes a problem after being hired, it impacts them. Instill confidence by assuring them that their choice of candidate will not carry any negative impact on their career.

Build referral time into the workday to show that referrals are a priority throughout the entire company.

✳ QUICK WINS

Record a short employee referral program introduction video. Record employees who have successfully made referrals talking about what they did with their referral bonus. This is a great story to share that makes the program and rewards more relatable. You can also record talent acquisition team members and senior leadership talking about why the referral program is so important for the growth and culture of the organization. Show this video to new hires as part of orientation and share it with existing employees, also reminding them of the bonuses available.

View example ERP intro videos that other companies have created here:
https://rlpt.co/ERPIntroVideos

Employees will care more if they feel empowered to convince prospective candidates to apply. Create an internal wiki or website for employees to contribute referral stories and access others. Not only does this motivate your team to seek out referrals, but also it shows the referred candidate how successful other referrals are.

2. HOW DO I EDUCATE EMPLOYEES ON WHERE TO SUBMIT REFERRALS?

Nothing kills motivation more than an overly complicated process for submitting referrals. However, even if you have the most straightforward process, your ERP will still fail if your staff doesn't know how to participate.

> **"** Employees want to know what happens to their referrals, when they're getting paid and the impact they're having on the business. As employees generally take the path of least resistance, make sure they know it's imperative they submit referrals in the right way to be eligible for bonuses and kept up-to-date on their referral's status."
>
> Matthew Perry, Vice President of Global Talent Acquisition, Conversant

One of the most common mistakes employees make is forwarding resumes to recruiters. This will lead to confusion and slow down your entire process.

Instead, teach them how to submit directly to your applicant tracking system (ATS). Start teaching this process on day one. Integrate ERP policies and procedure training into your onboarding process. Ideally, use video content to guide them through a demonstration of their full experience of the referral process.

STUDY: Our employees fully understand how to submit referrals

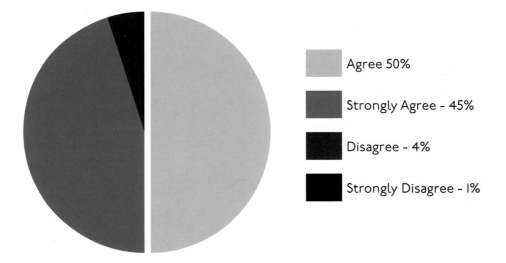

Agree 50%

Strongly Agree - 45%

Disagree - 4%

Strongly Disagree - 1%

However, this is not just a one-and-done training. Use lunch-and-learns to continually engage employees of all levels on how to participate in the referral process and keep them informed of any changes in your policies and procedures.

During your training sessions, distribute employee referral tool-kits that include content that describes the process, step-by-step. Your toolkit should also cover best practices for assessing candidates, expanding social media reach, and information about your company's hiring goals.

» EXPLORE FURTHER

View an example 'Making A Referral Guide' designed to educate employees around the referral process on page 117. (https://rlpt.co/MakingAReferralGuide)

3. HOW CAN LINE-MANAGERS HELP DRIVE EMPLOYEE PARTICIPATION?

The direct contact that managers have with employees gives them a great opportunity to push everyone to be the best referrers.

Employees should regularly receive reminders of the referral incentives they can earn. Use town hall sessions to open up intimate discussions among teams and their leaders.

Managers need to highlight hard-to-fill positions so employees understand what roles are the highest priority to scout for. Also, they should share real employee stories of those who successfully submit referred candidates. The story inventory is a great tool for managing these examples.

Encourage employees to ask questions during the town hall ses-

> **"** There's a certain amount of excitement generated by referrals that are coming from another star performer. There's an anticipation knowing that this is someone that our top guy has suggested and puts people in a different frame of mind. Even though it's the same screening process, there's more excitement to get a meeting on the calendar and this often results in a faster process."
>
> George Smallwood
> Director, Talent Acquisition, Ingram Content Group

> **"** Employee education is crucial. It is not just educating them on the tool that they're going to be using, it's educating them on the needs of the positions that the company is looking to hire for and what they're looking for in a great candidate. Educating the masses on the basic candidate criteria drives higher quality referrals. Getting the message out via line managers can really help with this."
>
> Rod Blomquist
> Talent Solutions Director, Skyline Group International

sions so they gain a better understanding of the process. This allows managers to reiterate the policies and procedures of the ERP and to teach employees about the correct channels to use when they need assistance with the program.

> " Instead of the program being a talent acquisition led initiative, it needs to be business led. That's a really important element of driving the awareness of the program and the buy-in. The follow-through is celebrating the successes, highlighting that the program is having a positive impact and that it matters. In previous organizations I've seen managers put in place KPIs around referrals – the programs are most successful when the business sees the value and the leaders help drive it."
>
> Bryce Murray, Managing Director, Talent Acquisition

Another effective strategy is called the 'gimme five' method. Asking for five names from employees of people they respect and would like to work with. This is a simple approach that is proactive and requires one-on-one interaction.

The simple truth is that your top performers are often busy and might overlook submitting referrals. Managers need to seek them out directly for a short period, such as after they return from an event or following a meeting. Booking 30 minutes in everyone's calendar once a quarter can be a good way for managers to make this a more defined and regular process.

Every employee interacts with talented people on a daily basis. This method cuts through the passive tactics from marketing your ERP and cuts directly to the chase.

✱ QUICK WINS

Ask line-managers to talk about the referral program for 5 minutes at their next team meeting. To take this a step further, have them ask everyone on their team to suggest one name by the end of the week for a specific hard-to-fill position on their team. To create a friendly sense of competition, you can have different line-managers compete to see who can generate the most referrals from their team within a 4 week period.

4. HOW DO I BRAND MY EMPLOYEE REFERRAL PROGRAM?

Employees are busy juggling their daily responsibilities associated with their role and balancing a healthy home life with their family. If your ERP is generic, it's forgettable.

Give your referral program a name and identity. Branding adds depth, making the program more recognizable and engaging.

Enlist the help of your marketing professionals and appoint them as brand administrators. They should take full ownership of the branding strategies and work closely with a content team.

> **"**We held a competition for employees to re-name the referrals program to build ownership and engagement. With the new name of the program, it was advertised everywhere on posters and cling-on window stickers in the high traffic areas of the building: break rooms, cafeteria, etc. There was weekly advertising with e-mails, jingles, and offering rewards throughout the referral journey."
>
> Dan Iazzetti, Senior Director, Talent Strategy, Engagement & Brand, Five Prime Therapeutics

Your content administrators will develop ideas, create unique content, and spread the message to your employees. Train these teams to work together and build a branding strategy that is fun and exciting.

> **"**We came up with the name 'Strong Connections - Put Your Network To Work' which is a play on words in line with our identity. We've used the name on promotional items like pens, notepads, magnets and posters at every retail center. We continuously come up with new ideas to help keep the program top of mind."
>
> Eric Clemons
> Sr. Manager – Employment Brand Strategies, US Cellular

STUDY: How do you brand and promote your employee referral program (ERP) to your employees?

Improve social media presence - 62%
Run internal advertisements - 52%
Create a name for the ERP - 48%
Praise top referrers publically - 38%
Hand out referral cards - 34%
Design and share a logo - 29%
Distribute 'referral profiles' for each department - 28%

One of the best examples of a successful branding campaign for an ERP comes from LinkedIn. Their talent acquisition team worked with their marketing department to create the name, Talent X. They raised awareness by running internal ERP advertisements that recognized their top referrers.

»EXPLORE FURTHER

Download and view page 16 of this *'Employee Referral Program Playbook'* to see how other companies have branded their employee referral programs: https://rlpt.co/EmployeeReferralProgramBranding

Add variety to your marketing campaigns by using themes and fun slogans to keep employees engaged.

5. HOW DO I GET EMPLOYEES TO FOCUS ON QUALITY REFERRALS?

"With spending so much time at work, people want to work and spend time with people who they like and respect. High performers will want to surround themselves with other high performers and that helps to create the company culture."

Dan Iazzetti, Senior Director, Talent Strategy, Engagement & Brand, Five Prime Therapeutics

If the incentive balance isn't right in a referral program, it can lead to large numbers of low-quality candidates being submitted. The best solution is training employees on what you look for in high-quality referrals.

Create candidate personas for hard-to-fill areas of your organization. This semi-fictional representation of your ideal candidate includes details on the candidate's experience, education, and skill set. It should also incorporate your 'big three.' The 'big three' are the three most important characteristics/values that align with your company culture. Employees will need to keep these in mind when assessing candidates for cultural fit.

> **"**Giving employees tools to quantify how strongly they are endorsing their referrals can help drive quality. There's a big difference between someone you loosely know and someone you've worked with previously at an organization. Strongly endorsed referrals are not only more likely to have the skills to perform the job, they tend to be greater cultural contributors to the organization also."
>
> Bryce Murray, Managing Director, Talent Acquisition

Host a candidate assessment workshop, where your talent acquisition team instructs employees on how to evaluate prospective referred candidates on their role fit, cultural fit, and other vital attributes.

Build mandatory candidate assessments into your employee referral process. This motivates your staff to confirm the level of quality their referral is before they submit a candidate.

> " We created a referral program video, one of the key themes was "matchmakers" because associates like to work with people they're comfortable with and people that they know – we like to share the message that 'what could be better than working with a friend?'. On the flip side, when a candidate is referred they're usually a better culture fit and they know that their referral's name is on the line, so they tend to stay at the company longer."
>
> Fatima Qizilbas
> Manager, Talent Marketing, LoyaltyOne

Set clear criteria for employees to rate the quality of each referral. One of the most effective ways of doing this is using several 'endorsement levels' to gather more context on the working relationship the employee has had with the candidate. Strongly endorsed candidates are those that employees have worked with in the past, weakly endorsed candidates are those that employees know very loosely (e.g., someone they spoke with briefly at a conference).

More advanced endorsements can include a 1-5 rating on the following criteria :

- Skills and knowledge: level of competence
- Cultural fit: alignment of values and beliefs
- Interest in the role: eagerness to take on job duties

- Interest in the company: enthusiasm for the mission and vision
- Overall rating: a general scoring of the candidate's ability to succeed in the role

Where possible, encourage employees to share examples of the candidate's work if it's relevant to the role.

Having a way for employees to track who they have referred and see how successful their candidates have been in moving through the screening process helps provide automated feedback on the quality of referral they are submitting. This motivates employees to find, evaluate, and submit the best of the best on a consistent basis.

✓ CHECKLIST: EDUCATION

☐ Our referral policy does not exceed I page in length and is easily accessible

☐ Employees know where to go to submit a referral

☐ Employees know where to direct questions around the referral program

☐ Employees know what success and participation based bonuses are available

☐ Line managers are responsible for educating their teams on the referral program

COMMUNICATION

"COMMUNICATION IS REALLY IMPORTANT. EXPLAINING NOT JUST WHAT YOU WANT TO DO, BUT WHY YOU WANT TO DO IT IS REALLY IMPORTANT, BECAUSE PEOPLE WANT MEANING."

SOPHIA AMORUSO

The success of your ERP depends on how well you effectively communicate with your employees. Raising awareness is vital to boosting participation and engagement.

In this chapter, we will cover the most commonly asked questions about communication:

How can you make employees aware of the program?

There is no set-it-and-forget-it approach, but it's important to keep this simple. We will explore our SIMPLE strategy for getting your staff excited about making referrals.

What channels are the most effective in getting the message across?

With so many online and offline channels, it's difficult to determine which ones are best for your program. We will look at how each channel is best used in promoting your ERP.

How often should you send employees communications around the referral program?

Daily reminders feel spammy, and annual events are too sparse. We will determine the best schedule to follow for communication about your ERP.

What are the most successful communications for driving participation?

Generalized messaging doesn't make much of an impact on your staff. We will discuss the value of segmenting your employees and using targeted messaging.

How can events be used to further promote engagement?

Sending email reminders and hanging posters isn't enough. We will offer insights on how various kinds of events can be used to boost ERP engagement.

I. HOW CAN YOU MAKE EMPLOYEES AWARE OF THE PROGRAM?

Promoting your ERP is one of the biggest obstacles you will face. Your communication strategy needs to be tailored to your culture and, most importantly, it should be simple to follow.

> **"**Give a full onboarding presentation that shares information and access to new employees. We see success in asking concise questions such as, "Who are the top 3 people in X field/industry?" as it helps focus them on the right people in what could be a large network of contacts."
>
> Jennifer Picard, Partner, KMA Talent Solutions

> **"**As part of group orientation we would ask new joiners to raise their hands and share who they were referred by. Referrals are such a huge thing, at the moment when new employees are coming into your company, it's a positive environment and the perfect time to embed the program as part of your culture."
>
> Rod Blomquist
> Talent Solutions Director, Skyline Group International

Here's a look at the SIMPLE strategy for raising awareness:

S - Set standards

- Build referrals into performance reviews so employees know it's part of their job. This shows encouragement and helps them overcome their reluctance to refer.

> **"**We will do a referral session with employees, get a pizza and help them match contacts from their social and professional networks. We educate them on the process to make them feel comfortable and help them find people in their networks that we think would be a good hire, that's worked really well."
>
> Shane Hicks, VP Global Talent, Epicor

I - Inform regularly

- Keep employees up-to-date when new jobs are posted. They won't know who to refer if they aren't aware of the current openings.

- Whenever new roles are posted, send your whole team a message with a link to the job description. Include social share buttons so they can post it to their social media accounts with one click.

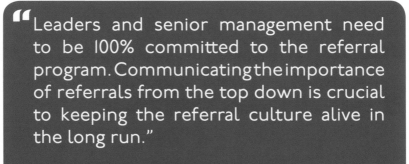

"Leaders and senior management need to be 100% committed to the referral program. Communicating the importance of referrals from the top down is crucial to keeping the referral culture alive in the long run."

Bethany Parthun
Corporate HR Manager, Talent, Evolution Hospitality

M - Meet individually

- One-on-one meetings give you a chance for a casual chat about your employees' networks. These source jams provide each employee with the nudge they need to review their networks and submit relevant referrals.

- Incorporate source jams into your onboarding process. This shows employees on day one that they are joining a recruiting culture where everyone is a talent scout.

STUDY: What actions do you take to make employees aware of your ERP?

Promote incentives

Host town hall meetings

New hire orientation sessions

Host demonstrations

Share success stories

Distribute policies and procedures

Host team events (banquets, lunches, etc.)

Send email reminders

Share training video

Percent of Respondents

P - Personalize messaging

- Target your communications to each individual based on their networks and job family. When you're looking for referrals in their department, send emails that address them by their name and highlight the benefit of a referral.

- For example, your subject line should read something like this: 'Let's work together to ensure you work with winners.' This reinforces why they benefit from submitting referrals.

L - Leverage all channels

- Don't just send emails or use a bulletin board. Invest in several channels, both online and offline. Otherwise, your messaging will be missed or forgotten. Your employee referral communications is an ongoing strategy that should connect with employees in several ways.

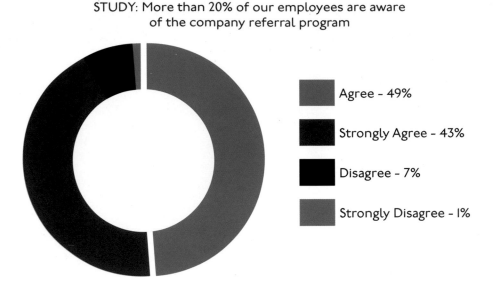

STUDY: More than 20% of our employees are aware of the company referral program

- Agree - 49%
- Strongly Agree - 43%
- Disagree - 7%
- Strongly Disagree - 1%

E - Engage with branding

- As we mentioned in the Education chapter, branding is essential. Generic ERPs are quickly forgotten.

- Get your marketing team involved with branding and running awareness campaigns.

> **» EXPLORE FURTHER**
>
> Watch this webinar titled *"Revamping your employee referral program in 90 days"*. Here you can learn how Dan Iazzetti used both online and offline communication methods to quickly increase awareness of their referral program: https://rlpt.co/RevampingIn90DaysWebinar

Hanging posters and sending reminder emails is just the beginning. Your communications strategy should take advantage of as many channels as possible.

> 90% of text messages are opened within the first 3 minutes. If you are able to get your employees opting-in to receiving text messages for your referral program, this can be a very powerful communication channel. **DID YOU KNOW?**

Online Channels

Email. When you're launching your program, send a company-wide email announcement. Include information about the employee referral process, qualities that make a high-quality referral, your incentives, eligibility rules, and why referrals constitute a significant benefit to your organization.

But don't stop there. Create an email strategy that regularly updates employees on your talent goals, future open postings, and tips on how they can best engage and attract their network.

Build an email communication campaign around a theme, like the 'Recruiting Roundup.' Praise your top referrers and announce which employees earn the most incentives.

> **"**Some ideas that have worked well for us are launch parties, hot job pushes, pizza and beer lunches, an open house of bring a friend to work, prizes, trips, etc. The most helpful and interesting one has been extending the referral program to the alumni network. Extended the reach to this group during the exit interviews and provided them cards and information on if they wanted to ever work for the company again in the future or suggest someone who would be a great fit."
>
> Jennifer Picard, Partner, KMA Talent Solutions

Build an email communication campaign around a theme, like the 'Recruiting Roundup.' Praise your top referrers and announce which employees earn the most incentives.

SMS. Text messaging is the best direct channel to each employee. Send out reminder messages when new jobs are posted. Also, use text messaging to promote hiring events and share information about your referral program leaders.

For example, if you're hosting a competition, send out monthly text messages to show who the top referrers are.

Video. The most significant trend in content is video - and for good reason. People prefer watching videos over reading. In terms of marketing, four times as many consumers would rather watch a video about a product than read about it.[15]

Use video to give your employees a step-by-step demonstration of how they can submit referrals. Introduce this video in the on-boarding process, but continually share it so employees know exactly how to submit referrals.

Offline Channels

Posters. These can be especially valuable if you're using engaging visuals. Text-heavy posters won't grab the attention of too many employees.

Break up your text and incorporate images that align with your messaging. For example, include images of cash or other winnable prizes on posters that center on your incentive policies.

> **"**We like to put together posters campaign that are edgy, innovative and rich with graphics. One campaign we used which was showing the roots of a tree and it was all about growing the next organizational tree. We also try to help employees visualize what they can do with the reward. The message is think about what referring a friend can help you earn in the real world, in much more tangible terms."
>
> Shane Hicks, VP Global Talent, Epicor

Consider using fun themes to make them more memorable. If your campaign theme is 'Build a Team of Champions,' use images of athletes crossing a finish line or holding trophies.

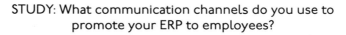

> **"**We've done a Friday Afternoon Club where we took a cart around and gave snacks and beverages in exchange for referrals. We also had a raffle that each referral would be entered into to win a week long 'Fuze Cruise'.**"**
>
> Nell Heisner, Partner, Foundation Talent

Flyers. Use these to distribute to employees at events or in the workplace. Flyers are often smaller, so keep your text concise. Align these with your campaigns.

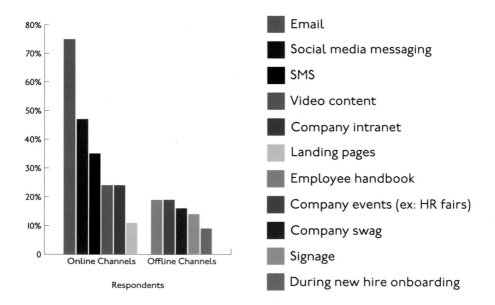

STUDY: What communication channels do you use to promote your ERP to employees?

- Email
- Social media messaging
- SMS
- Video content
- Company intranet
- Landing pages
- Employee handbook
- Company events (ex: HR fairs)
- Company swag
- Signage
- During new hire onboarding

STUDY: How effective is your communications strategy for raising awareness around the referral program?

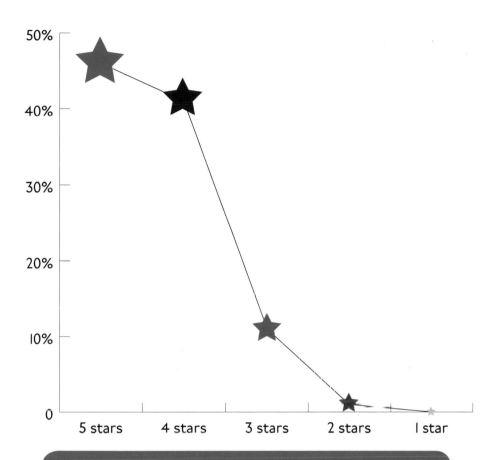

» EXPLORE FURTHER

Download and view this *'Employee Referral Program Playbook'* to see a wide selection of ways to promote your program internally. These include example email campaigns, posters, video formats, social media messages and more: https://rlpt.co/EmployeeReferralsPlaybook

Scratchcards. Give these away immediately when an employee gives you a referral name as a lead. This instant chance of winning a prize is a great way to get employees excited about the program.

Branded Swag. From T-shirts and bags to mugs and water bottles, there are numerous possibilities for branding company swag. Encourage employees to wear company-branded gear.

✱ QUICK WINS

Make referral program posters.
A great way to build momentum behind a program is to start small and take action immediately. There's no better way of doing this than a small scale offline marketing campaign.

You can edit these customizable referral program poster templates in PowerPoint and start putting them up in high employee foot-traffic areas today: https://rlpt.co/ReferralProgramPosterTemplates

Distribute swag at company events and use them to recognize your top referrers. For example, reward your leading referrers with shirts that say 'Elite Referrer.' They can wear these shirts to team events, or display an 'Elite Referrer' trophy on their desk.

3. HOW OFTEN SHOULD YOU SEND EMPLOYEES COMMUNICATIONS AROUND THE REFERRAL PROGRAM?

Messaging and tactics are vital to effectively promoting your ERP.

However, you also need to know how to time your promotions.

Campaigns. Coordinate different campaigns at least once every quarter with a unique theme. These campaigns could revolve around incentives.

For example, run a raffle for a big prize your employees wouldn't likely spend money on, like a Caribbean cruise or a helicopter trip over Napa Valley. Highlight limited-time incentives, like a 2x cash bonus during a campaign period.

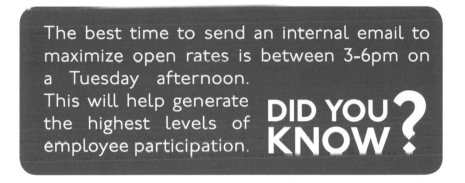

The best time to send an internal email to maximize open rates is between 3-6pm on a Tuesday afternoon. This will help generate the highest levels of employee participation. **DID YOU KNOW?**

Emails. Send emails with educational content every quarter. They should summarize your most recent employee referral campaign and offer tips to make your employees better talent scouts and referrers.

Here are a few email templates to use for education emails:

- **Wrap Up.** This email summarizes your previous campaign and shares success stories from your top referrers. It also includes a sneak peek at your upcoming campaign.
- **Top Referrers.** This includes the current tally of your leaderboards for your referral competition. It consists of the best referrals submitted and quotes from the top referrers. Also, highlight the incentives your top referrers won.
- **Quick Tips.** Offer actionable solutions to common prob-

lems your employees may face, like assessing candidates for cultural fit.

> **"**Communications around the referral program started during the recruiting process. We mentioned the referral bonus to all candidates we interviewed on the first call and positioned it as a benefit of working at the organization. We noticed a higher success rate for candidates who referred someone else during their own screening process."
>
> Luan Lam, VP Talent, Harness

> **"**For us, regular communication is the most important part of a successful referral program. Whether it's specific campaigns we are running or just communication around the importance of the referral program, it needs to flow from leadership all the way down to employees. We normally have monthly campaign announcements that go out to the whole company. When we're running a targeted campaign, we'll usually send out a reminder every two weeks."
>
> Nadine Lou, Talent Acquisition Specialist, MarketSource

Reminders. Technology is the best tool for keeping your staff in the know. Use push notifications through text messaging or internal social network channels, like Slack. These can be instant reminders when a job is posted.

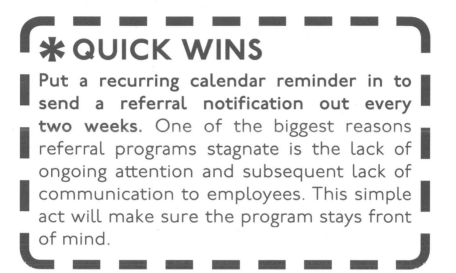

✳ QUICK WINS

Put a recurring calendar reminder in to send a referral notification out every two weeks. One of the biggest reasons referral programs stagnate is the lack of ongoing attention and subsequent lack of communication to employees. This simple act will make sure the program stays front of mind.

Also, host Company Growth meetings every quarter to teach your staff about relevant jobs. This is especially beneficial if you have several hard-to-fill positions. Educate employees on the specific skills you're looking for as well as how to assess for these more complex roles.

4. WHAT ARE THE MOST SUCCESSFUL COMMUNICATIONS FOR DRIVING PARTICIPATION?

The best way to encourage more employees to participate in your ERP is to target your communications.

Generalized messaging usually falls flat. Employees want to be spoken to on an individual basis. Of course, hiring great colleagues would benefit the whole company, but how would it impact the individual?

Start by segmenting employees by grouping them by their job family and their networks. Promote specific talent needs to employees who work in the same job family.

> **"**We use a combination of company-wide and targeted campaigns. Where we see the most success is running campaigns at the individual hospital level; we partner with the leaders in those locations to drive participation and focus attention by adding specific openings along with a temporarily increased incentive."
>
> Brooke Glennon, Associate Director, Recruitment Marketing & Operations, Encompass Health

Chances are, your software engineers in a particular city will know where to find other engineers in that city and have a better idea of what constitutes a high-quality candidate.

> **"**Create a strong call-to-action. Why are you asking me reach out to my network? Is it to hire talent, is it to help diversify, is it to grow our salesforce aggressively to take number one market share? Help the employees understand the bigger picture of why they're doing this."
>
> Kevin Benton, Head of Americas Talent Acquisition & Global Executive Search, McAfee

Tailor your communication strategies to each employee segment. For example, when you need to hire new customer service representatives, notify your customer service team and show them how they can play a part in strengthening their team. Describe what attributes the ideal candidate would have and ask for their input as well.

> **"**An original advertising campaign we did in the past featured former colleague names on the walls for a pizza party of people we were looking to target. Since people arrived and came in with no context, they immediately reacted and it energized their thought process. By doing this we hired an SVP, 2 Directors, and entry level positions of 2-3 years experience."
>
> Jennifer Picard, Partner, KMA Talent Solutions

For example, GoDaddy wrote an employee referral program poster in computer code. It sparked curiosity with their talent and their coders decoded the message, which was a simple call to action -- refer a coder in your network to us. This spoke directly to a specific segment of the staff (coders) and started a conversation in the office.

5. HOW CAN EVENTS BE USED TO FURTHER PROMOTE ENGAGEMENT?

Events are essential in getting employees engaged and thinking like a talent scout. When you bring the whole team together, you will get everyone on the same page.

Here are some events to host:

Bring-A-Friend events. Invite your employees, their friends, and their families to a career fair for your organization. This encourages your staff to reach out to their networks.

> "We have a HR Summit every year where our 60 HR Directors come in for two and half days of training. What's so impactful is that we hand out individualized reports for how the referral programs are performing in their locations along with the company performance overall. Because we're handing them very specific personalized information, it's exciting - they want to see how many referrals they've had, how many job shares, what their participation levels are. We also hand out referral program swag and have rewards for the best performing location in each region. It's always one of the busiest booths at the events and really helps drive participation throughout the year."
>
> Chandler Cougill
> Recruitment Strategy Consultant, Encompass Health

> "Within 90 days of starting we invite new employees to breakfast. We ask them about their experience of applying to roles, onboarding and acclimatization. We ask 'if you haven't referred someone, why haven't you?', if you have, 'how's your experience been?' 80% of employees show up to this and it's great way to assess the overall candidate and employee referral experience."

Matthew Perry
Vice President, Global Talent Acquisition, Conversant

> "During sponsored lunches we had a team of 10 recruiters with iPads collecting referrals from people queuing for food. This was a great opportunity to educate employees on the program at a time when they were receptive to hearing about it. We also had a table for the referral program at our benefits day where employees could spin a wheel to win prizes when they submitted a referral name."

Luan Lam, VP Talent, Harness

If you invite several high-quality candidates, conduct speed-networking, where everyone visits stations for short interactions. Break up stations by department and team.

Also, host short interviews that connect the best of the best with your hiring team. This face-to-face interaction helps build positive rapport fast and expedites the hiring process for referrals.

Cultural hiring parties. These parties can be more informal and focused on celebrating what makes your culture unique. Send out an open invitation for everyone's networks and host workshops and presentations to educate potential candidates about your culture.

✱ QUICK WINS

Host a referral lunch.
One of the easiest and most universal applicable ways to generate referrals quickly is to give away free lunch in exchange for referrals. One way of doing this is to provide free pizza if employees give you three referral leads. The immediacy of the reward makes this a very fast and effective way to collect referrals.

Showcase your values, the mission, your products/services, and what kinds of employees help your company grow. Theme the party in a creative way that's unique to your organization.

For example, an outdoor recreation company should host a group hike or a summer picnic party in a local park. This event aligns with the culture and the brand.

Referral scavenger hunt. This is a great exercise for your employees to do at networking events. Teach them how to expand their network and connect with industry colleagues.

Sign them up for a professional organization. Then assign them a scavenger hunt during the organization's events. This hunt will include information about what candidates make strong cultural fits and sets employees a goal of meeting a certain number of people.

✅ CHECKLIST: COMMUNICATION

- ☐ We tell employees about the referral program as part of new employee onboarding

- ☐ We use a combination of online and offline communication channels

- ☐ We run at least one referral campaign a quarter

- ☐ We have C-level support behind the program and messaging

- ☐ We are able to send messages out to certain employee segments

ELEMENT 5

TECHNOLOGY

"SHARING IS GOOD, AND WITH DIGITAL TECHNOLOGY, SHARING IS EASY."

RICHARD STALLMAN

The most successful ERPs are simple for employees and employers alike. The foundation for a simplified program is technology.

In this chapter, we will examine the most commonly asked questions about using technology in your ERP:

How should employees submit referrals?

Submitting referrals needs to be streamlined and simple for your employees. We will look at the role technology plays in delivering a positive experience to make referral submissions easy.

How do social networks help generate more employee referrals?

Your talent likely has great social capital. This is essential in your ERP. We will determine how to get your staff to make the most of their networks through various channels, like social media.

How does matching technology help personalize the employee experience?

Matching candidates to jobs doesn't need to be a long process. We will explore how matching technology helps your staff scour their networks for the best fit.

How can we automate bonus reporting to payroll?

Automation frees up time and resources for your team. We will show you how to leverage technology to simplify reporting and ensure your employees receive the bonuses they deserve.

How does technology help give employees more transparency over their referred candidates?

Transparency breaks down the most prominent barriers with your employees. We will share solutions to avoiding the 'referral black hole.'

On average 40% of employee referrals are made via mobile devices. In some industries such as retail, where mobile devices are the primary device for accessing the internet, this number is up to 70%. Make sure your employees can make referrals on mobile devices!

DID YOU KNOW?

1. HOW SHOULD EMPLOYEES SUBMIT REFERRALS?

Building the employee experience of the referral program is a major challenge. When it comes to submitting candidates, your employee experience requires three essential aspects:

- It's user-friendly
- It's accessible
- It's mobile-friendly

> **"**For us one of the main challenges, was the ease or should I say lack of ease of the process. We worked through our applicant tracking system and it was cumbersome and confusing, this ultimately resulted in people either going around the referral policy or not referring at all."
>
> George Smallwood
> Director, Talent Acquisition, Ingram Content Group

The best solution is giving them access in their pockets. Over three-quarters of Americans (77 percent) say they own a smartphone.[16]

STUDY: How often do you receive feedback that it's too complicated for employees to refer someone through your referral program?

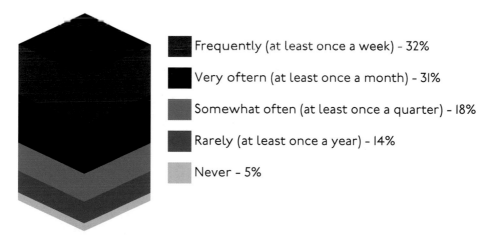

Frequently (at least once a week) - 32%

Very oftern (at least once a month) - 31%

Somewhat often (at least once a quarter) - 18%

Rarely (at least once a year) - 14%

Never - 5%

Smartphones are more integrated into our lives than ever before and it's impacting the workplace - 82 percent of employees with smartphones keep them within eye contact at work.[17]

Give them access on their mobile devices. Instead of jumping through hoops, your employees can refer a candidate with a few clicks. The more accessible the referral submission process is, the more time they have to submit more quality referrals.

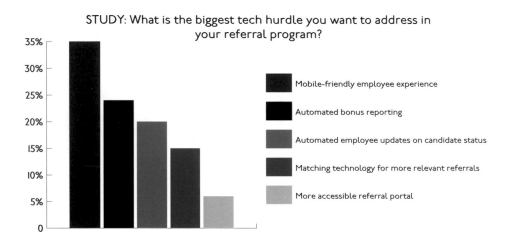

STUDY: What is the biggest tech hurdle you want to address in your referral program?

- Mobile-friendly employee experience
- Automated bonus reporting
- Automated employee updates on candidate status
- Matching technology for more relevant referrals
- More accessible referral portal

Focus on building a simple portal so your employees can easily navigate it. They should be able to log in, search for open jobs, link to their social media accounts, match connections to open roles, and easily refer someone to the ATS.

> **»EXPLORE FURTHER**
> Read this *'Mobility and Recruiting'* whitepaper to learn how the proliferation of mobile devices are impacting the recruiting technology landscape:
> https://rlpt.co/MobilityWhitepaper

Thanks to social media, each employee can potentially reach hundreds of connections with the click of a button. Their social networks are one of your best resources for talent.

> **"**For me, it's the UI and UX is really important. It has to look and feel intuitive from a user perspective. One of the reasons that we made the change from using our standard ATS functionality to a dedicated referral platform was that it was just so difficult to use. And, let's be frank, it was really ugly as well. First of all, an intuitive UI and the ability to share and socialize and evangelize jobs to your social networks as part of the tool is crucial. This helps turn our employees to brand social evangelists, in our case that's 3,800 employees into 3,800 recruiters."
>
> Shane Hicks, VP Global Talent, Epicor

Here are a few ways to get more referrals from your staff's networks:

Job Sharing. Your staff can share an opening once you post it. Make this easy by adding social share buttons to your portal.

Also, write the content you want them to include when they share the job opening. Train them to personalize their shares as well. This way, they add some personality and avoid sounding spammy.

Employer Brand Content Sharing. Successful employer branding strategies center on creating great content about the company culture and celebrating the employee experience. As you generate employee testimonials, shoutouts, behind-the-scenes stories, and more, encourage your employees to share this content with their networks.

You can also host contests to encourage your employees to celebrate your employer brand. For example, host a Twitter contest where they need to share why they love their job through emojis or coordinate an Instagram competition for funniest story posts that sum up their workday.

Contact matching. Sync employees' social media contacts with your ERP platform. Then use matching technology that automatically aligns contacts with open jobs based on experience and skills.

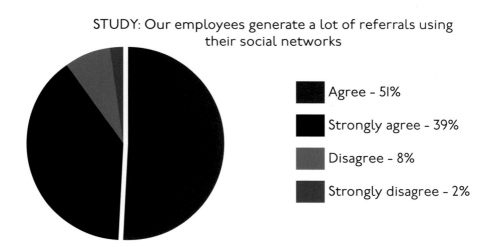

STUDY: Our employees generate a lot of referrals using their social networks

- Agree - 51%
- Strongly agree - 39%
- Disagree - 8%
- Strongly disagree - 2%

Combining Social Recruiting with Referrals

Extend your ERP into social recruiting by leveraging your staff's social media presence in these ways:

Twitter. Train your staff on how to make the most of this short-form platform. Whenever you post a job and announce it to your staff, give them a guide on what keywords to use as hashtags in their tweets. Hashtags reach users who might be looking for specific job keywords, like '#engineering' or '#projectmanagement."

Facebook. Encourage your employees to join Facebook Groups and Pages. When they become a part of an online community, they're expanding their networks and finding more talent to screen. Show them how to reach out in a professional manner.

LinkedIn. Similar to Facebook, employees should be engaging with LinkedIn Groups associated with their professions. They can also search through several degrees of connections, previous co-workers, and fellow alumni.

The most crucial step for employees to remember is to make a personal connection with their referrals. A name isn't as good as a positive rapport. When they develop relationships, they know more about the candidate and how they will fit the culture and role.

3. HOW DOES MATCHING TECHNOLOGY HELP PERSONALIZE THE EMPLOYEE EXPERIENCE?

The algorithms used by job boards match candidates with positions instantly. Your ERP portal should be no different.

Matching technology can be deployed in a variety of ways, such as:

Resume to job matching. If an employee doesn't know which role their contact would be a good fit for, resume to job matching provides appropriate job recommendations based on their resume. This avoids employee submitting the candidate as a 'general' or 'non-job-specific referral.'

Contact to job matching. Employees can upload their professional network contacts and quickly see which of them would be a good fit for a given job requisition. With employees often having hundreds, if not thousands, of contacts, this allows them to quickly find those that may be the most relevant to refer in.

> **"**Allowing employees to upload their professional network and easily see contacts that would be a good fit for certain roles, makes the matchmaking process much faster and easier. There's a huge opportunity to increase social reach."
>
> Brad Cook, VP Talent, Teradata

Job to employee matching. 80% of referrals are made for roles within the same department and within 50 miles of the employee's location. Serving up a shortlist of jobs that employees are most likely to refer to makes the experience much more tailored to the individual employee and means they are more likely to take action. These matched jobs can be delivered via email, SMS or within the referral portal.

Past referral to new job matching. Large organizations can generate thousands of referrals relatively quickly. With 5 to 1 being a good referral-to-hire ratio, that still means the majority of referrals are not successful. These referred candidates may be suitable for future roles, however. Past referral matching technology can maximize the value of these referrals and suggest them to recruiters for future requisitions that open up.

> **"**A good referral program requires a strong foundation. A technology platform can do this by facilitating communication between the employee, the candidate and the recruiting team. This creates a seamless and transparent experience for everyone involved."
>
> Michelle Sargent
> Head of Strategic Partnerships, KRT Marketing

With employee attention being more finite than ever, it's crucial to ensure a personalized experience. Generic communications and unsophisticated technology risks frustrating employees who generally have limited patience for non-core work. Matching technology not only makes the process easier for employees but can often get them excited at the prospect of trying out innovative technology. A leading edge referral technology sends a strong message to employees that the ERP is important enough to warrant a dedicated platform.

»EXPLORE FURTHER

Watch this 3 minute video entitled '*The Top 5 Most Useful Referral Technology Features*':

https://rlpt.co/Top5MostUsefulFeatures

Technology is automating more processes in the workplace, which takes care of a lot of menial tasks. For example, timesheets and payroll are moving away from paper-based processes.

There's no reason referral incentives can't be automated. Talent acquisition teams shouldn't be bogged down with managing referral payouts using spreadsheets. Investing this time in further marketing the referral program instead delivers multitudes of ROI.

> **"**We recognize that after a new employee has signed a contract, it's really important that we introduce them to the referral program. In certain regions, we will ask for their referrals before they join, paying the bonus out once they've started. It's really important we have a payment process in place so the moment they join were able to reward them and keep the positive momentum going."
>
> Shane Hicks, VP Global Talent, Epicor

With manual reporting, there is also a much higher risk that reward payments will slip through the cracks. When employees have to chase up their bonuses, this can often cause frustration and lack of trust that they will be paid out for future contributions to the referral program.

Technology can simplify bonus reporting to payroll. The common use-cases include:

Handling duplicate referrals. Informing employees immediately if they have submitted a referral that is already in the database and that they will not be eligible for a bonus.

Eligibility criteria. For example senior executives, HR, and recruiters not being eligible for bonuses.

Probation periods. Ensuring both the employee and referred candidate are still at the organization after the probation period number of days.

Tiered referral rewards. Automatically tracking different tiers of employee referral bonus depending on the seniority of the role.

Point tracking. Companies that have gamified their programs may wish to give employees points for certain referral actions. These points can be reported on and linked to other corporate initiatives such as recognition schemes.

STUDY: How do you track employee referral bonuses?

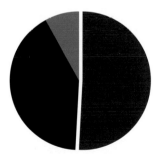

■ With automatic reports to payroll - 51%

■ Manually, using a spreadsheet - 41%

■ Employees are asked to track bonuses - 8%

One of the biggest obstacles keeping employees from referring is a lack of transparency on many fronts. It can cause a lot of confusion around:

- How to submit referrals through the portal
- How to keep updated on candidates's progression
- How or when you will receive rewards
- How a referral impacts your career
- How a referred candidate is treated

Your best solution is to focus on both visibility and communication.

> "It's valuable to give the employee an immediate 'thank you' after they've made a referral. An immediate thank you that reiterates the value of referrals. Then it's important to tell the employee what happens next in the process - here's what bonus you're eligible for and here's where you can see the status of your candidate. Thankful, informative, and rewarding."
>
> Kevin Benton, Head of Americas
> Talent Acquisition & Global Executive Search, McAfee

The 'referral black hole' is your worst enemy. Employees submit a candidate they believe in, but then they hear nothing back. No follow-ups. No feedback. No information on where the candidate is in the hiring process and no reward or recognition for their efforts.

> **"**It's hard to put a monetary value on a good candidate and employee experience. We've had the feedback from employees that with more transparency, the black-hole is taken away. That positive experience dividends in long term employee engagement levels."
>
> Matthew Perry
> Vice President, Global Talent Acquisition, Conversant

This black hole effect makes employees feel cheated out of the incentives you promised them. They also feel invalidated. After all, they likely put a great deal of thought into who best fits the open role. They even took the time to reach out to the candidate with job information.

> **"**Produce a diagram of your employee referral process highlighting when each touchpoint occurs within the process. This will make it clear to both the employees and recruiting team what the experience should be, helping set expectations and creating accountability on the business side."
>
> Justin Copp
> Senior Manager, Global Talent Acquisition, PayPal

Keep them in the loop with automatic updates on the status of their referred candidate. Show them what stage they advance to and where they fall off.

Share detailed feedback on why the candidate didn't work out. Don't criticize them for their choices. Instead, praise them for their efforts and express gratitude.

Also, automate updates on the incentives. Tailor your communications so employees know what they can expect to receive and when.

If they don't qualify for the rewards, explain why they don't and offer tips on how to receive the reward with future referrals.

Transparency is vital in every aspect of your ERP. Be upfront from the start to establish trust with your staff.

For example, offer a clear explanation when you request access to their data, such as their LinkedIn or Facebook networks. Describe what you're doing with that information and why it benefits the company and the employee. Otherwise, they might worry you're stealing their network data.

»EXPLORE FURTHER

Download and view page 32 of this '*Employee Referral Program Playbook*' to see '24 questions to ask when purchasing employee referral technology': https://rlpt. co/EmployeeReferralsPlaybook

✓ CHECKLIST: TECHNOLOGY

☐ We have a referral portal for employees to make referrals that is also accessible on mobile devices

☐ The portal is on a URL that is easy to remember e.g. (*yourcompanyname*)referrals.com

☐ Matching technology personalizes the employee referral process

☐ There is automatic reporting to payroll for employee referral incentives

☐ Employees are automatically kept updated on their referred candidates status

THE 6TH ELEMENT: ACTION

"KNOWLEDGE WITHOUT ACTION IS FUTILE"

ABU BAKR

If we were to identify a single reason why employee referral programs fail to reach their potential, it's a lack of action. More specifically, it's the lack of ongoing attention to the program and the assumption that it can be left on autopilot.

Many talent acquisition teams we've worked with have recounted experiences of having focused on the referral program for a few months and then, with another project taking priority, it falling off by the wayside and being left to stagnate. Equally, those organizations that have been the most successful didn't necessarily have the strongest employer brand or most lucrative incentives; they were the most dedicated to continually improving the program over time. Referral programs need someone to take ownership and in-line with the elements discussed in this book, need a framework to measure success. If you continue to spend time on fine-tuning your program, ensuring it is marketed internally and kept fresh with interesting incentives, you are guaranteed to see more success in the number of referred hires being generated. The real challenge can often be ensuring the program is prioritized above everything else competing to find time on your calendar.

A successful referral program comes with a change in organizational mindset. It's imperative that your organization understands that a referral program is more than just a policy. It's a dynamic network that feeds off the activities and successes of employees, requiring a dedicated individual or team to deliver a consistently engaging experience. Surprisingly few initiatives within an organization are accessible by the entire employee base, giving referral programs a substantial opportunity to impact the culture.

If you are serious about improving your referral program, having someone accountable for the program's success is the catalyst that creates ongoing positive change. They will build momentum and be responsible for ongoing action, opening the doors to implementing everything we have discussed in this book. If that person is you, then we wish you the best of success on your journey.

#1 EMPLOYEE REFERRAL PROGRAM TIP

We asked some of the top talent acquisition and recruitment professionals what is the number one piece of advice for running a successful referral program. If there is one thing to take away from this book, here it is:

> "Employee engagement is the most important element! The common slogan is, "Great people know great people." When employees feel like they are part of a good culture, they will evangelize the brand. It's not enough to have the best tools or programs, it all comes down to employee engagement."
>
> Jennifer Picard
> Partner, KMA Talent Solutions

> "The focus on making the process as clean, simple, and transparent as possible has been so successful for us, we've been able to go from 21 percent to 40 percent of hires through referral."
>
> George Smallwood
> Director, Talent Acquisition, Ingram Content Group

> " Number one, employee engagement. Number two, avoid a black hole. Number three, allowing some level of self service to the employees to understand the status of the referral."
>
> Kevin Benton, Head of Americas
> Talent Acquisition & Global Executive Search, McAfee

> " Anonymize the candidate source before being passed onto recruiters and hiring managers. We've seen this actually improves conversion rates from referrals."
>
> Grant Weinberg
> Global Talent Acquisition Leader, Gilead Sciences

> " Just do it! Without any hesitation, the key is to just do it. Don't get caught up in the policies or guidelines. By getting started, it starts the process sooner of getting higher quality candidates in the door. It's a no-brainer!"
>
> Dan Iazzetti, Senior Director,
> Talent Strategy, Engagement & Brand, Five Prime Therapeutics

> Transparency in the referral process breeds trust, no referral program will do well without it."
>
> Matthew Perry
> Vice President, Global Talent Acquisition, Conversant

> It comes down to transparency and communication. Letting employees know that their referrals aren't going into a "black hole." No one likes to refer anyone if they think the referral is going nowhere. If a company can recognize and give acknowledgement and information to their employees, people are more likely to feel like the company cares and that the company knows what they are doing."
>
> Nell Heisner, Partner, Foundation Talent

> Maximize the enterprise socialization of your program - Get out often, keep the ideas fresh and ensure variety."
>
> Justin Copp
> Senior Manager, Global Talent Acquisition, PayPal

"Make it more about activity and not holding employees responsible for people getting successfully hired in the system. When it's about activity, they'll be more likely to participate, whether it is a job share or just making a simple referral. But, if you hold them responsible for someone actually having to get hired, we did see a drop-off especially with part-time employees, because obviously a lot of the hiring process is out of their hands. If a company is looking to increase their number of referrals, I would say base it around activity. It could be as simple as starting with employees activating a referral account and making them feel like they're included."

Nadine Lou, Talent Acquisition Specialist, MarketSource

"Communication, communication, communication. Employees are frequently interacting with potentially great candidates. The challenge is getting them into the right mindset to continuously evaluate whether folks would be a good fit for the organization."

Bethany Parthun
Corporate HR Manager, Talent, Evolution Hospitality

> " Be different, make it fun and run frequent temporary campaigns. Make it competitive and think outside of the box to get your message in front of employees."

Melissa Ngo-Harris, Recruiting Manager, Aptos Retail

> " Give the program an identity and constantly communicate it in fun and engaging ways to keep employees interested."

Eric Clemons
Sr. Manager – Employment Brand Strategies, US Cellular

> " Make your referral program easy and make it accessible. If associates are easily able to log into a platform to refer their candidates, you'll see a larger number of quality candidates submitted. When associates have roadblocks logging-in and the program is complicated, this will limit participation in the program."

Fatima Qizilbas, Manager, Talent Marketing, LoyaltyOne

> "Run the referral program like a business – invest time and energy, market it and always make sure you follow up on the candidates coming in."
>
> Luan Lam, VP Talent, Harness

> "Make sure whatever precedent you set through the referral program as to the company's employer value proposition, it's something you can live up to throughout the candidate experience. Ensure your referral program is consistent with that overall employer value proposition as an organization."
>
> Bryce Murray, Managing Director, Talent Acquisition

> "Be deliberate in promoting your program and always consider your program from your employees' perspective. Work to exceed what you'd want your experience to be were you in their position, especially as it related to timely and thorough communications."
>
> Joe Shaker Jr, President, Shaker Recruitment Marketing

> **If you have a referral program, make sure there is the right technology in place to make it a great experience."**
>
> Michelle Sargent, Head of Strategic Partnerships, KRT Marketing

> **Keep the program fresh. Many companies will set their referral fees, setup their portal and leave it on cruise control. The program really needs ongoing management and attention to keep employees fully engaged."**
>
> Neil Costa, Founder & CEO, HiroClix

> **Create buy-in. Often the biggest challenge isn't getting HR, Talent Acquisition or Recruiting to understand the importance of a referral program, it's getting senior leadership behind the program. Be prepared to educate the leadership team on the importance of a referral program – that usually comes down to higher quality candidates, saving money and the high return on investment versus other sources."**
>
> Rod Blomquist
> Talent Solutions Director, Skyline Group International

GRADING YOUR REFERRAL PROGRAM

Here we've assembled the corresponding checklists for every element. Over the next three pages, you can quickly grade your employee referral program by checking off the 25 items and see how you compare against other organizations.

<5. Begin by creating a strong foundation with clear objectives and a solid referral policy.

5-10. On par with the majority of organizations, identify a single element to optimize.

10-15. Focus on Quick Wins for ways to boost performance across elements.

15-20. In-line with the top 5% of organizations, identify which gaps are the easiest to fill.

20+ Best-in-class, keep it up!

The sum of all checked boxes over the following three pages is your score! Additionally, you can calculate your score off of the last page of each element section.

- [ ] We know what percentage of hires we currently receive through referrals as a source

- [ ] We have a defined target percentage of hires we want through referrals over the next 12 months

- [ ] We have a defined budget of how much we want to spend on the referral program in the next 12 months

- [ ] We have an understanding of which departments/locations we need to generate more referrals in

- [ ] We have strategic recruiting goals (diversity/veteran/campus/employer branding) and can tie this to the referral program

- [ ] We offer cash rewards for successful rewards (success based bonuses)

- [ ] Our probation period for referred hires is no more than 90 days

- [ ] We offer non-cash rewards for employees submitting qualified referrals (participation based bonuses)

- [ ] We have the flexibility to run campaigns with temporary bonuses (gift-cards/raffle prizes/charity donations)

- [ ] We use social recognition to highlight top performing referrers

- [ ] Our referral policy does not exceed I page in length and is easily accessible

- [ ] Employees know where to go to submit a referral

- [ ] Employees know where to direct questions around the referral program

- [ ] Employees know what success and participation based bonuses are available

- [ ] Line managers are responsible for educating their teams on the referral program

- [ ] We tell employees about the referral program as part of new employee onboarding

- [ ] We use a combination of online and offline communication channels

- [ ] We run at least one referral campaign a quarter

- [ ] We have C-level support behind the program and messaging

- [ ] We are able to send messages out to certain employee segments

- [ ] We have a referral portal for employees to make referrals that is also accessible on mobile devices

- [ ] The portal is on a URL that is easy to remember e.g. (*yourcompanyname*)referrals.com

- [ ] Matching technology personalizes the employee referral process

- [ ] There is automatic reporting to payroll for employee referral incentives

- [ ] Employees are automatically kept updated on their referred candidates status

APPENDIX A: REFERRAL POLICY

Download: https://rlpt.co/SampleEmployeeReferralPolicy

Sample Employee Referral Policy

Purpose: Our employees are our most important asset and we know that no one knows our business like our current employees. That's why we developed our Employee Referral Program: to encourage our amazing employees to get involved in helping to build our company by referring your talented friends, family and former colleagues to roles here at <company name>. And to thank you for your involvement, you will be rewarded for your successfully hired referrals through cash bonus opportunities.

Incentives:

If your referred candidate is hired, you as the referring employee will receive $x,xxx if all eligibility requirements are met (see below for eligibility.)

Notes:
• The Talent Acquisition Team may increase bonuses for specific hard-to-fill roles at any given time.
• You will receive your bonus in one-lump sum and it is subject to standard payroll and tax withholdings.
• There is up to a 60-day processing period for bonus payouts.

Eligibility:

• All permanent employees are eligible to participate in the Employee Referral Program.
• We welcome interns and contractors to participate in the program but they are not eligible to receive a referral bonus.
• If your referred candidate is successfully hired, you will be eligible to receive a referral bonus after their 60th day of employment.
• The referring employee must be an active employee at the time of payout.
• The hired referral must be an active employee at the time of payout.
• All jobs are bonus eligible unless otherwise noted.
• While you may refer candidates to internships (and we encourage you to do so!), referrals to internships are exempt from the program and are not bonus eligible.
• Candidates referred who are current employees of <company name> are not bonus eligible. Current employees who are interested in moving within the company should click here to learn more about our Internal Mobility program.
• Once a candidate is referred by an employee, the first referring employee owns that referral for a period of 365 days. Candidates who are referred by multiple employees will be accredited to the first-referring employee for the entirety of the referral ownership period.
• Final decisions regarding the eligibility for a referral bonus will be decided by the Talent Acquisition Team.

How to Refer:

All employee referrals must be made through our Employee Referral Tool (powered by RolePoint.) To do so, visit this URL: companyname.rolepoint.com. Important: Make sure you are logged in before making your referral! Once you make your referral, you will receive a confirmation email that your referral was successful. You can track your referrals in your "History/My Referrals" page within your referral account.

Questions?

Send your questions to <email>. We'll respond back to inquiries within x-working days.

APPENDIX B: REFERRAL GUIDE

Download: https://rlpt.co/MakingAReferralGuide

Start Here
You will need to login to your Referral Account

View Open Jobs
All of our open jobs are found on the portal

Make a Referral
1. Share on social media
2. Direct Referral
3. General Referral

Candidate Applies
1. Browses jobs through link
2. Receives email with direct link
3. Receives email to browse jobs

Candidates will receive an email application received confirmation and the referral details will be stored in Haufe.

Once your candidate is received by the recruiting team, they will review their CV. Your candidate will be in the "NEW" status at this time. Follow the workflow below to see how your referred candidate moves through the recruiting process.

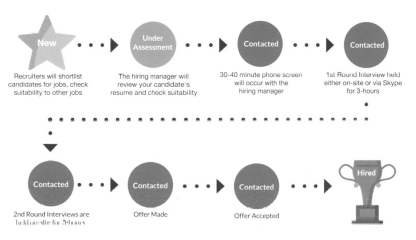

New
Recruiters will shortlist candidates for jobs, check suitability to other jobs

Under Assessment
The hiring manager will review your candidate's resume and check suitability

Contacted
30-40 minute phone screen will occur with the hiring manager

Contacted
1st Round Interview held either on-site or via Skype for 3-hours

Contacted
2nd Round Interviews are held on-site for 3-hours

Contacted
Offer Made

Contacted
Offer Accepted

Hired

Additional Need-to-Know Information:

Archived
At any point during the interviewing process, if your candidate is not selected, they will receive feedback either via email or by phone based on the stage. The candidate will also move to the "Archived" status, which you will be able to view when logged into your account.

As a reminder, all referrals should be made via the Employee Referral Portal. You may access the portal by visiting: YOUR COMPANY NAME.RolePoint.com. #JoinCOMPANYNAME

Remember to check the status of your referrals by visiting the "History" page within your account.

Questions? Contact: recruiting@yourcompany.com
You may also view the COMPANY Referral Program FAQs by visiting: COMPANY FAQ SITE

APPENDIX C: BUSINESS JUSTIFICATION

WHY INVEST IN EMPLOYEE REFERRALS?

Referrals are hired faster: Referrals are the #1 fastest time to fill (29 days for referrals, 39 days for job boards, and 45 days for career sites)

Referred candidates convert at a higher rate: Referrals are #1 and are hired at a rate of 1 out of 4 applications. Compare that to an average applicant to hire ratio of 1 out of 18 from all sources.

Referred hires perform better: Hires from referrals produce approximately 25 percent more profit impact than hires from other sources. A referral from a top performer who is hired will produce nearly three times more profit impact for the firm compared to the referred worker from a below average performer.

Referrals are a better cultural fit: 70% of employers feel referrals fit the company culture and values better.

Referrals stay longer: Referrals are #1 at 46% retention after one year (compared to 33% from career sites and 22% from job boards).

EMPLOYEE BENEFITS
- Easy referral submission
- Mobile accessibility
- Relevant job suggestions
- Social sharing & matching
- Engaging gamification
- Clear feedback loop

TALENT ACQUISITION BENEFITS
- Increased participation
- Automated employee updates
- Higher quality referrals
- Automated bonus reporting
- Campaign & content support
- Detailed analytics

WHAT IS THE ROI OF A REFERRAL PROGRAM PLATFORM?

Increased referral hires: Increase referral rates from 25% to a minimum of 35%

Increased participation: Increase employee participation to reach a minimum of 40%

Focus on the hardest to fill positions: Increase referrals for our hardest-to-fill positions by 300%

Improved employee experience: Reduce number of employee inquiries by 80%

Time saving: Save 20 hours per week managing the referral program

ENDNOTES

1	Sources of Hire 2017 report from SilkRoad
2	Linkedin Global Recruiting Trends 2017
3	Jobvite 2012 IG
4	Jobvite 2012 IG
5	Linkedin Ultimate List of Hiring Stats
6	Sources of Hire 2017 report from SilkRoad
7	Top Echelon stats
8	Sources of Hire 2017 report from SilkRoad
9	Linkedin Global Recruiting Trends 2017
10	Jobvite 2012 IG
11	Linkedin Global Recruiting Trends 2018
12	Linkedin Global Recruiting Trends 2017

13   https://www.hubspot.com/company-news/hubspot-launches-30000-referral-program-for-developers-and-designers,   https://www.brazen.com/blog/archive/career-growth/refer-a-friend-15-employee-referral-programs-that-offer-serious-cash/

14   https://www.amazon.com/Work-Rules-Insights-Inside-Transform-ebook/dp/B00MEMMVB8,   https://business.linkedin.com/talent-solutions/blog/employee-referrals/2016/4-steal-worthy-secrets-of-top-employee-referral-programs

15   https://animoto.com/blog/business/video-marketing-cheat-sheet-infographic/

16   http://www.pewresearch.org/fact-tank/2017/06/28/10-facts-about-smart-phones/

17   https://www.careerbuilder.com/share/aboutus/pressreleasesdetail.aspx?ed=12/31/2016&id=pr954&sd=6/9/2016